Contents

The Washington Papers/125

Czechoslovakia

Charter 77's Decade of Dissent

Janusz Bugajski

Foreword by Walter Laqueur

Published with The Center for
Strategic and International Studies
Washington D.C.

PRAEGER

New York
Westport, Connecticut
London

Library of Congress Cataloging in Publication Data

Bugajski, Janusz, 1954–
   Czechoslovakia, Charter 77's decade of dissent.

   (The Washington papers, ISSN 0278-937X; vol. XV, 125)
   "Published with the Center for Strategic and
International Studies, Washington, D.C."
   Includes bibliographical references and index.
   1. Czechoslovakia – Politics and government –
1968– . 2. Czechoslovakia – Intellectual life –
1945– . 3. Civil rights – Czechoslovakia –
History – 20th century. 4. Dissenters – History –
20th century. I. Title. II. Series: Washington papers ; 123.
DB2228.7.B8 1987   943.7′04   87-2435
ISBN 0-275-92769-5 (alk. paper)
ISBN 0-275-92770-9 (pbk. : alk. paper)

Library of Congress Catalog Card Number: 87-2435
ISBN: 0-275-92769-5 (cloth)
        0-275-92770-9 (paper)

First published in 1987

Praeger Publishers, 521 Fifth Avenue, New York, NY 10175
A division of Greenwood Press, Inc.

Printed in the United States of America

The paper used in this book complies with the Permanent
Paper Standard issued by the National Information Standards
Organization (Z39.48-1984).

P

Foreword

The story of Czechoslovakia during the last two decades is perhaps sadder than that of any other East European country. This does not refer primarily to the economic situation, which, admittedly, is far from brilliant. It is a case of stagnation rather than rapid decline. Investment has decreased. Czechoslovak industry has fallen behind and finds it increasingly difficult to compete in world markets; the foreign trade profile of the country has been compared with Third World regimes. The outlook for the future may be grim, but currently there are no acute shortages as far as essential commodities are concerned, and the elderly rulers resist even the modest reforms preached by Mr. Gorbachev, fearful perhaps that any reform in Czechoslovakia would have far-reaching consequences. They are fearful even of the activities of a few young jazz musicians.

The real tragedy, however, is political and cultural. Russia, after all, never knew freedom in its long history except for a very short interregnum; Albania, with due respect, was never one of the centers of European and world culture. But Czechoslovakia had a great deal of autonomy even under Hapsburg rule, and after World War I it was a parliamentary democracy with as much freedom as any country in the world. Ironically, it was one of the few countries with a substantial, legal Communist Party. Culturally, Prague was for a long time one of the centers of European culture. Its university is the oldest in Europe. *Don Giovanni* was first performed in this city, which was (or became) the home of some of the greatest composers and writers in the annals of mankind.

Then there came the German occupation, and, after a short democratic interval, a new dictatorship. As the Slansky trials were to show, it was extremely repressive even by East European standards. In the 1960s there were some moments of hope, but the invasion of the fraternal armies ended the dreams about "Communism with a human face."

Today Czechoslovakia is a cultural desert. True, it has produced some magnificent tennis players, but not all of them have remained in their country of birth, and in any case, this is hardly the achievement of the political and social order. Politically and culturally the contrast between present and past is all the more palpable in view of the rich democratic tradition of the country. Yet even in this darkness some lights have been shining, encouraged perhaps by the lessons of Czechoslovak history and the knowledge that foreign rule may not last forever. Among these lights, uniting the most democratic, progressive, and forward-looking forces, the subscribers to Charter 77 ought to be mentioned in first place. Very little is known in the West about their struggle, and it is hoped that this excellent book will fill this void.

Walter Laqueur
Center for Strategic and International Studies

January 1987

About the Author

Janusz Bugajski is a research associate, working with Professor Walter Laqueur at the Center for Strategic and International Studies in Washington, DC. During 1984 and 1985 he was a senior research analyst at Radio Free Europe in Munich, West Germany. Prior to that he served as a consultant and researcher on Polish affairs for BBC television in London.

Bugajski was born in England and obtained a B.A. Hons. from the University of Kent at Canterbury, England and an M. Phil. in social anthropology from the London School of Economics and Political Science. He has published in several international journals including The *Washington Quarterly, Political Communication and Persuasion, Encounter,* and the *Economist* and is a frequent contributor to various national and international newspapers. He is a contributing author to *Soviet/East European Survey* (Duke University Press, 1985, 1986, and 1987) and was a regular writer on current events in Eastern Europe for Radio Free Europe *Situation Reports* and *Background Reports* during 1984 and 1985.

Acknowledgements

In addition to the important archival sources mentioned in the text and footnotes, I would like to mention the invaluable assistance provided by my research interns at the Center for Strategic and International Studies — Patrice McMahon, Heidi Liszka, David Janssen, Michael Evans, and John Forman in particular.

THE WASHINGTON PAPERS

... intended to meet the need for an authoritative, yet prompt, public appraisal of the major developments in world affairs.

Series Editors: Walter Laqueur; Amos A. Jordan

Associate Editors: William J. Taylor, Jr.; Thomas Bleha

Executive Editor: Jean C. Newsom

Managing Editor: Nancy B. Eddy

President, CSIS: Amos A. Jordan

MANUSCRIPT SUBMISSION

The Washington Papers and Praeger Publishers welcome inquiries concerning manuscript submissions. Please include with your inquiry a curriculum vitae, synopsis, table of contents, and estimated manuscript length. Manuscripts must be between 120–200 double-spaced typed pages. All submissions will be peer reviewed. Submissions to *The Washington Papers* should be sent to *The Washington Papers*; The Center for Strategic and International Studies; 1800 K Street NW; Suite 400; Washington, DC 20006. Book proposals should be sent to Praeger Publishers; 521 Fifth Avenue; New York NY 10175.

Introduction

This study of a decade of dissent in Czechoslovakia helps shed some light on the possibilities, limits, and prospects for political opposition in communist states. Although Charter 77 has not evolved into a mass movement, on the scale of Poland's Solidarity, it has managed to survive longer than other dissident groups in neighboring Soviet bloc countries. This can be explained largely by its focus on peaceable, open, and law-abiding activities, rooted in international human rights conventions, and the involvement of a sizable number of alienated Czechoslovak intellectuals who successfully weather the storms of official repression.

The most important development in the campaign for democratic reform in Czechoslovakia since the 1968 Prague Spring has been the creation, in January 1977, of the human rights campaign inaugurated by the Charter 77 founding declaration. Charter 77 is not a mass protest movement and has not posed a direct political challenge to the Czechoslovak regime. Nevertheless, as an essential ingredient of an authentic campaign for fundamental political, civil, economic, cultural, and national rights, the Charter's existence undermines the principles of the totalitarian communist system.

Charter 77, together with its various offshoots and related campaigns, has survived the regime's attempts to silence all opposition through imprisonment, intimidation, harassment, and other forms of persecution. The chartists have laboriously monitored and documented the systematic violations of human and civil rights, exposed the acute social, economic, and ecological problems facing the country, and recommended practical remedies to introduce effective reforms. They have publicized their activities at home and abroad and helped to underscore the shortcomings and hypocrisy of the authorities. Charter 77 has maintained cohesiveness, despite the wide spectrum of political orientations and ideologies its signatories represent. The defense of human rights has provided them with an enduring joint platform for their activities.

To estimate fully the long-term impact of Charter 77 is difficult, but during the last decade the human rights campaign has helped to preserve the spirit of the 1968 reform movement and Czechoslovak traditions of democracy and liberalism. The charter has opened up a new chapter in the struggle for civil liberties and national independence. Equally important, Charter 77 again underscores the fact that the Soviet-imposed system of government in Czechoslovakia has no social mandate. The system ultimately rests on coercion and the subjugation of individual and collective rights and freedoms.

1

History and Context

Czechoslovakia is a communist state in the heart of central Europe. The country's political system is based internally on the dominant role of the Czechoslovak Communist Party (CPCS) and externally on its subordination to the Soviet Union. The Communist Party strictly supervises the executive and administrative organs of government; the party controls the economy, the armed forces, citizens militia, secret police, the judiciary, and the mass media; and it directs all official labor unions, professional organizations, and other social and cultural institutions. As a member of the Warsaw Pact military-political alliance and of the Council for Mutual Economic Assistance (CMEA), Czechoslovakia is fully integrated into the Soviet bloc of East European states.

The Czechoslovak Communist Party seized power in February 1948 in a bloodless coup d'état that was characterized by unconstitutional procedural methods that eliminated free elections. The takeover was backed by detachments of the party-controlled workers militia, and by the ever-present threat of the Soviet Red Army. Several years of Stalinist terror, during which hundreds of political opponents were executed and tens of thousands more imprisoned, followed the coup. Nationalization of industry, be-

3

gun in 1945, was completed and farming was collectivized as the new regime sought to establish a stranglehold over all sectors of society.

The relative thaw throughout Eastern Europe following Stalin's death and Khrushchev's revelations about the abuses wrought by the "cult of the personality" eventually spawned the "Prague Spring" of 1968. Reformists within and outside the party attempted to construct "socialism with a human face," in which the democratic participation of ordinary citizens in social, economic, and political life would play an important role. A nationwide movement for wide-ranging reforms was awakened, and various independent initiatives began to challenge implicitly or explicitly the party's monopoly of power. In August 1968, Warsaw Pact forces from five Soviet bloc states, directed by the Red Army, invaded the country and proceeded to extinguish the democratic revival. A Charter 77 statement issued on the seventeenth anniversary of the Soviet invasion declared:

> Even according to a resolution of the Presidium of the Central Committee of the CPCS, made during the night of August 20/21, this happened against the wishes and knowledge of that organ, the President of the Republic, the government, and the National Assembly, and in breach of the principles of international law, including the provisions of the Warsaw Pact.[1]

Gustáv Husák was installed as general-secretary of the redisciplined CPCS in 1969 and appointed head of state in 1975, clearly against the wishes of society. The blatant use of force and manipulation, illegal under international law and the country's own constitution, was clothed in "communist legality." According to the Brezhnev doctrine, the Soviet Union and other socialist states have the supreme right and, in fact, the obligation to intervene in the internal affairs of any East bloc member whenever the Kremlin considers socialism to be under threat therein.

The period since 1969 has witnessed a policy of "normalization," in which the absolute monopoly of the party in all spheres of public life was restored, society was pacified, and independent groups and movements were crushed. The long overdue plans to reform the political and economic system were aborted, and a wave of repression swept through education, the mass media, the administration, and cultural life. An estimated 1 million people were affected when workers in a whole range of occupations lost their positions or were demoted. Many of the victims and their families still suffer from official discrimination to this day.[2] The CPCS itself was purged of reformers, losing about a third of its membership—more than half a million people. Since 1968, more than 150,000 citizens have fled the country. In many instances these were young, well-educated, and skilled individuals.[3] The militia and security service apparatus of the CPCS was greatly expanded in manpower and equipment and has never been reduced. The party reimposed its monopoly of information and its control over the mass media by handpicking and carefully screening all editors and journalists and by suppressing alternative sources of information.

An unwritten social contract was forged between rulers and the ruled during the 1970s, whereby citizens were guaranteed a tolerable material standard of living and a reasonable degree of privacy in return for their nonparticipation in politics and decision making. The party leadership thereby was assured of the passivity and depoliticization of most of the population and could provide the greatest rewards to its most loyal functionaries and bureaucrats. According to one founder-signatory of Charter 77 during this period:

> Economically determined conformism vis-à-vis the system took on a pronounced form of social corruption . . . in the sphere of consumption and distribution, the production process, and all working activity, social services, state administration . . . and public and political life in general.[4]

Since the late 1970s, the highly centralized, overbureaucratized, and inefficient economy has diminished the government's ability to live up to its side of the bargain. Living standards have been stagnating and falling, while shortages of certain goods are becoming more frequent. Some economists maintain that real wages were lower by about 2 percent in 1983 compared to 1978, while real personal consumption in 1983 fell below the 1981 level. Prospects look bleak for the modernization of industry, and the cost of new investments has grown drastically during recent years. The overcentralized and ossified system of economic planning is becoming more cumbersome, and the economy is unable to respond to demands for efficiency and technological development.

Despite a chronic need for structural changes, the prospect for improvement through far-reaching economic reforms remains slight. Party leaders evidently fear that reforms would undermine their political control. Intensive police surveillance and party supervision continue to keep the lid down on any potential organized public dissent. Pressing preoccupation with material goods for the average family as well as a widespread feeling of resignation clearly place limitations on expressions of protest. The regime even seems to tolerate widespread corruption, blackmarketeering, and moonlighting, because such activities act as important safety valves by satisfying some of the material needs the system itself cannot provide. According to a recent Charter 77 document, society is riddled with corruption, bribery, the abuse of power, shoddy workmanship, theft, cynicism, demoralization, and widescale waste of human and material resources. These harmful phenomena

> can only be overcome by society as a whole, only as a result of people's spontaneous initiative. But the mechanics of our society provide no outlet for individual initiative. The willingness, enterprise, and creativity that would benefit all of us, will not come about until people sense that they are trusted. . . . The way things

are today, with rigid institutionalization, coercion, and bureaucratic interference, is not conducive to trust.[5]

It is against such an unpromising background that Charter 77 emerged. For a decade it has campaigned to rectify these conditions.

2

Origins and Aims

Origins of Charter 77

The Husák regime crushed the 1968 reform movement within and outside the Czechoslovak Communist Party through stringent political vetting and the dismissal of more than a quarter of a million people from government posts. Nevertheless, passive opposition to the government persisted among some sectors of the population. In the early 1970s, small groups made attempts to organize effective pressure for reform.[6] These often were led by expelled party members who had not abandoned all hope for peaceful change. Their weakness lay in the fact that they constituted a minority within the ranks of the purged, had little popular support or influence, and were divided among themselves as to strategy and tactics. The most well-known group, the "Socialist Movement of Czechoslovak Citizens," closely identified itself with the Prague Spring reform movement and included a number of prominent CPCS reformist politicians. Following the publication of their "Short Action Program" in January–February 1971, several leaders of the group were arrested and later sentenced in the summer of 1972. The organization suffered a severe blow from which it was subsequently unable to recover.

Other pro-reformist groups during the 1970s included the Student-Worker Coordinating Committees, the Movement of Revolutionary Youth, Communists in Opposition, the Czechoslovak Movement for Democratic Socialism, the Civil Resistance Movement, and an assortment of smaller opposition groups. By the mid-1970s, however, the opposition had become isolated, ineffectual, and deeply divided on such issues as compromise with the regime and the legality of their actions. Security forces also hounded and effectively suppressed group members.

The production and distribution of *samizdat* material, text produced outside official censorship, has a long history in Czechoslovakia, dating back to the Communist coup in 1948. There was a resurgence of such publications after the 1968 invasion and again in the mid-1970s. Independent publishing grew noticeably at these times, and a regular stream of protest letters were dispatched to government officials by disaffected intellectuals. *Samizdat* texts took various forms—petitions, letters, commentaries, reports on persecution, periodicals, and even full-length books. Much of the material found its way abroad, because the dissidents were determined to refocus world attention on Czechoslovakia under "normalization" at a time when public interest in the West seemed to be waning. Several appeals describing the repressions in Czechoslovakia were sent to organizations in Western Europe and North America, together with scholarly analyses of the country's predicament. Although the achievements of the opposition before 1977 were limited, its activities, particularly in independent publishing, preserved a measure of continuity in the reform movement. Its perseverance contributed to the formulation of Charter 77, which provided a common platform and a concrete purpose for the various strands of the opposition.

The breeding ground for Charter 77 lay in the dissatisfaction and alienation after 1968 of many prominent intellectuals who were barred from public life and could not

engage in their professions. Disgruntlement was fanned by
the repressive nature of the Prague regime, which prohibited freedom of speech and association by making all social
and cultural activities subject to strict official supervision
and censorship. Nevertheless, the authorities were unable
to silence all the critical voices. An early indication that
human rights could became a rallying point for dissent
came with the *samizdat* publication of the "Ten Points Manifesto" on August 21, 1969, signed by several eminent reformists. Point four of the manifesto expressed concern
about the banning of the "Society For Human Rights," particularly active during the Prague Spring, and called for the
implementation of international pacts on civil, economic,
and cultural rights.

The ferment among purged intellectuals was given a
significant morale boost by international developments after 1975. In August 1975, the Helsinki Final Act, which
concluded the Helsinki Conference on European Security
and Cooperation (CSCE), reaffirmed the United Nations
covenants on human rights, which the Czechoslovak government signed in 1968. The Helsinki Final Act provided
for follow-up sessions to the CSCE and stipulated that each
signatory party would give legal status domestically to the
"Ten Principles" of the act. In October 1976, Prague formally legalized the Helsinki accords by publishing them in the
official collection of "Laws of Czechoslovakia." Although the
act did not constitute a binding international treaty, the 35
participating states undertook to abide by the ten principles, which include "respect for human rights and fundamental freedoms, including the freedom of thought, conscience, religion, or belief." Czechoslovakia's participation in
the accords underscored claims by the Czechoslovak opposition that it was not engaging in criminal or subversive
activities; it legitimized oppositionist appeals and condem-
nations of human rights abuses and provided them with a
clear-cut campaign platform in the international arena.

Another direct spur to the creation of Charter 77 was
supplied by the official campaign against the rock music

band, the Plastic People of the Universe, and against other young people during 1976. A trial in Prague in September 1976 involving the incarceration of four young musicians for performing nonconformist songs led to public protest. An open letter from 10 former lawyers who had been deprived of work since 1969 declared that government measures were "the latest in a series of administrative interventions limiting and invalidating civil rights and freedoms, especially freedom of artistic creation, scientific research, and freedom of expression."[7] The campaign for the defense of the musicians brought together various discontented groups in an informal but practical way and indicated that common action was indeed possible around specific civil rights issues. The government's publication of the human rights covenants encouraged dissidents to envisage achieving a modicum of success.

Charter 77 was essentially the product of debate among disenfranchised intellectuals and reform Communists purged from the CPCS after 1969. It is unclear exactly who conceived the idea of the charter, but the initial signatories, including writers, academics, professors, journalists, former politicians, party functionaries, technicians, students, and a spattering of blue-collar workers, represented a fairly broad spectrum of ideological positions. The instigators of the charter sought the broadest possible movement of citizens in defense of fundamental civil liberties. The Charter 77 text was made public on January 6, 1977 and contained 243 signatures. The document was drafted during the Christmas period of 1976, and the signatures were appended when it was finalized. Three of the initiators, Pavel Landovský, Václav Havel, and Ludvík Vaculík, intended to deliver it personally to the offices of the government, the federal assembly, and the Czechoslovak press agency, but they were apprehended by the police while about to do so. As a result, the authorities came into possession of the Charter 77 text even before it was formally issued. During the following few weeks it was given widespread domestic and international publicity.

The Charter's Objectives

According to its founding declaration, dated January 1, 1977, "Charter 77 is a free, informal, and open community of people of different convictions, different faiths, and different professions, united by the will to strive, individually and collectively, for the respect of civic and human rights."[8] The chartists stressed that they were not establishing a political organization, because Charter 77 had no rules, statutes, permanent bodies, or formal membership and did not provide a basis for oppositionist political activities.[9] Furthermore, the charter did not avowedly propose a program for political reform, "but within its own sphere of activity it wishes to conduct a constructive dialogue with the political and state authorities."[10]

Charter 77 urged the involvement of citizens in guarding civil rights, underlining that this crucial work could not be left to the state authorities alone. To legitimize this initiative it called upon the support of the United Nations Universal Declaration of Human Rights, the International Covenant on Civil and Political Rights, the International Covenant on Economic, Social and Cultural Rights, and the Helsinki Final Act. The chartists made a forthright appeal for dialogue with the Communist Party authorities,

> particularly by drawing attention to various individual cases where human and civil rights are violated, by preparing documents and suggesting solutions, by submitting other proposals of a more general character aimed at reinforcing such rights and their guarantees, and by acting as a mediator in various conflict situations which may lead to injustice, and so forth.[11]

The document listed several specific areas in which international and domestic laws were violated by the government: discrimination in employment and education, official control of the communications media, publishing and culture, the curtailment of religious freedom, the nonexistence of numerous basic civic rights, and the state's systematic interference in the private lives of citizens.[12] The charter stressed the serious limitations placed on freedom of association, in which individuals or organizations have no recourse to any institution outside of party control in interpreting their rights and duties. Charter signatories presented themselves as the instigators of a citizens' initiative to create precisely this kind of independent body.

The Charter 77 founding declaration pointed out that despite the Prague government's ratification of the Helsinki Final Act, conditions in the country were not improving. In effect, the chartists were demanding that the regime obey its own laws and respect the international obligations it had freely undertaken. They were also describing the realities of "normalized" Czechoslovakia to the outside world and encouraging concerned Czechoslovak citizens to join them in their strictly legal endeavors.

The appearance of Charter 77 was psychologically important, because it breached the barrier of fear deliberately cultivated by the government. The avoidance of ideological or political overtones and the commitment to act openly and strictly within the law evidently broadened the charter's appeal. The chartists harbored few illusions that the authorities would respond promptly to their propositions by implementing all the relevant rights or negotiating with the signatories. They calculated correctly, however, that the campaign would not be ignored by officials. Whether the reaction of the regime proved to be positive or negative, they reasoned, Charter 77 could initiate far-reaching social and political changes in Czechoslovakia or at least create a climate in which such transformations could eventually materialize — when international and domestic conditions became more favorable.

Strategies and Tactics

From the outset there were a number of pressing internal issues requiring resolution among the charter signatories, issues that concerned the nature and direction of the campaign. Although working compromises have always been achieved, which enable the movement to continue functioning, disputes have occasionally surfaced, particularly when official repressions have periodically subsided. In general, during severe anti-charter drives, the movement has been able to close its ranks and present a united front. To understand the internal workings of Charter 77 and the strategies adopted vis-à-vis the regime, it is useful to examine briefly the major issues that have contributed to making the movement into a forum for discussion as well as a human rights initiative.

The question of whether the chartists should function openly or clandestinely was resolved relatively early on. It was decided that secretive and anonymous activities would be counterproductive, because they would provide the regime with a clear-cut excuse for strangling the charter at birth—by imprisoning all known oppositionists and dismissing it domestically and internationally as a "terrorist organization" or an "anti-state conspiracy." On the other hand, by operating openly and disclosing the names of its signatories from the outset, Charter 77 could depict itself as a completely legal, human rights initiative without subversive intentions, based on international covenants and Czechoslovak law. Also, by declaring itself in favor of "constructive dialogue" with the government, Charter 77 could further disarm the regime's offensive.

If the authorities declared a willingness to engage in talks, the chartists reasoned, a major breakthrough would be achieved. On the other hand, if they refused to countenance any discussions and suppressed the movement, the repressive nature of the regime, despite its endorsement of human rights conventions, would again be brought to world attention. Although most of the charter's supporters were skeptical that the government would readily negotiate or drastically change its policies, they felt that to offer a dialogue was an important starting point for demonstrating the charter's peaceful and realistic motives.

The important issue of whether Charter 77 should develop into a political organization or a loose nonpolitical pressure group has preoccupied many of its signatories. Although there was initially an informal agreement to keep the movement apolitical, following the government's crackdown in early 1977 opinions began to diverge on how the charter's aims could be achieved most effectively and whether additional goals should be included. A comprehensive internal debate on this question involved more than 200 signatories and supporters. Many people, especially those of a more radical Left persuasion, asserted that an overtly political approach should be adopted by forging a definite political program, an organizational framework, and a formal membership. The majority, however, particularly the so-called ex-Communist reformers and Christians in the movement, opposed such moves and warned that this could contribute to the charter's downfall.

It is doubtful that the diverse groupings and ideological tendencies within Charter 77 could reach a binding consensus or a common political program without splitting the movement into a number of minute and ineffectual factions. Such measures also would have provided the regime with additional justification for eliminating its opponents. A compromise solution eventually emerged, whereby Charter 77 would uphold its original aims and operational methods but encourage independent initiatives on other issues, especially those that were not avowedly political.[13]

An important early compromise arrangement, which contributed to resolving internal disputes, consisted of the appointment of three official "spokespersons" from each of the major political-ideological orientations within Charter 77—the "reform communists," the "independent liberals," and the "Christians." Their official function was to sign and authorize all Charter 77 declarations and to represent the movement in dealings with outsiders. The three signatories were changed annually, though some of them subsequently served on two or more occasions during the course of the decade, particularly following periodic police crackdowns and arrests.

Discussions about the politicization of the movement have arisen periodically during the past decade. In early 1979, several dissident intellectuals and Christian activists criticized the Charter spokespersons for becoming too political and losing touch with the majority of signatories and supporters. Consequently, the three newly appointed spokespersons conducted meetings with numerous signatories and decided that ties among chartists should be encouraged to allow internal democracy to operate more effectively. Conditions in the country, however, made it difficult to maintain regular contacts; holding large meetings was extremely risky and time consuming. Also, because charter spokespersons often needed to react swiftly to events, they had little time for broad consultations. The fact that Charter 77 survived the often heated internal disputes, while only a dozen or so individuals reportedly have withdrawn their signatures in the past 10 years, indicates that a general consensus has existed regarding methods, directions, and priorities.

Since the early debates, the chartists occasionally have reaffirmed that they are not an alternative political team seeking power but rather a pressure group of responsible citizens. The charter imposes no organizational discipline or ideological orientation upon its signatories and activists, but does seek to promulgate independent political thinking in Czechoslovak society. Despite the efforts of the signers to avoid developing the movement into a political opposition, in a totalitarian state any form of prohibited protest automatically becomes an oppositionist act and a political challenge to the regime. This is how the Communist authorities have interpreted Charter 77. During an interview with Norwegian journalists in March 1984, the three charter spokespersons of the day, Václav Benda, Jiří Ruml, and Jana Šternová, underlined the danger in classifying Charter 77 according to political yardsticks; they confirmed, however, that

we are aware that in the absence of independent political structures, our "solidarity in elementary human and

civic decency" becomes a political act with significant
political consequences.[14]

Other vexing questions have preoccupied the chartists—including whether to opt for a restricted or mass
membership. Everyone was at liberty to sign the charter at
any time, but because the movement was not a structured
organization, there was little need to involve masses of people in its operations. Furthermore, the chartists evidently
did not rate their success according to the number of signatories, but by their effectiveness in influencing the authorities and stimulating autonomous citizens' activities. Although initially opposed by many ex-Communists, the
majority of the chartists reasoned that the best compromise between restricted and mass membership was to encourage various cultural and educational pursuits among
the population parallel to those run by the state. The more
circumscribed aims of Charter 77 were to be maintained,
however. The government also helped to provide an answer
to the question of size by isolating the chartists from the
masses.

Chartists periodically have suggested disbanding, but
because of the lack of agreement on a suitable alternative,
the consensus holds that if no one monitored the violations
or campaigned for a proper defense, the struggle for human
rights and civil liberties could suffer serious reversals. The
chartists have regularly addressed their own critics on several perennial issues. In answer to recent charges that Charter 77 was feeling the effects of so many years of exertion
and appeared to be flagging, the chartists pointed out that
their long-term strategy was not tied to "the romantic ideal
of feverish revolutionary tumult or hectic activism" but "determined, calm, patient, rational, and economical" work:

> The aims of the Charter are of a long-term nature, and
> in fact can never be fully attained. Hence the need for
> modest and patient work, for quiet, matter-of-fact, un-
> ostentatious activity that consumes only the optimum
> amount of energy. We would consider it preferable if

Charter 77 issued only one good and thorough document each year rather than made itself noisily noticeable every day, paying for all this clamour with slapdash and superficial statements, or with action that aimed at no more than publicity and popularity.[15]

3

Activists and Supporters

Charter 77 Spokespersons and Signatories

An impressive array of prominent intellectuals has served as Charter 77 spokespersons during the past decade. In recent years, however, lesser known and younger individuals have been replacing their imprisoned, harassed, or exhausted colleagues at the forefront of the human rights campaign. To examine the driving force behind the charter, it is helpful to look briefly at the biographies of all Charter 77 spokespersons from 1977 through 1986.[16] They are listed in alphabetical order, and in parentheses after their name are the years in which they served as spokespersons, either for the entire year or only for part of a year.

Rudolf Battěk (1980) (b. 1925, sociologist.) Battěk was a member of the Sociological Institute of the Czechoslovak Academy of Sciences until 1969 and a former member of the Czechoslovak National Council. On the first anniversary of the Soviet invasion he cosigned a petition on the perils of normalization and spent the next 13 months in prison. He was sentenced to three and a half years in prison in 1972 for participating in a campaign to inform citizens of their legal right not to vote in parliamentary elections. An early charter signatory and cofounder of the "independent social-

19

ist" group (which supports the program of the Socialist International), Battěk was arrested twice during 1980. He was convicted in July 1981 on subversion charges and sentenced to seven and a half years – reduced to five and a half years in October 1981 following an appeal. His health deteriorated rapidly in prison. Conditionally released in October 1985, he was placed under "protective surveillance."

Václav Benda (1979, 1984) (b. 1946, philosopher and mathematician.) Benda was expelled from Prague's Charles University for his political and religious views and dismissed from his post as a computer programmer for signing Charter 77. Arrested in May 1979 and tried in October 1979, he was charged with subversion and sentenced to four years in prison. He is a practicing Catholic, and his prose has been published unofficially. Since his release in May 1983, he has been detained several times, particularly in connection with his protest against the stationing of Soviet missiles in Czechoslovakia. Benda was discharged from his job as a stoker in November 1985 and is currently unemployed.

Jiří Dienstbier (1979, 1985) (b. 1937, well-known radio journalist.) A former foreign correspondent and editor of Czechoslovak Radio in the United States and Far East, he was dismissed from his post in 1969 and expelled from the CPCS and the Union of Czechoslovak Journalists. He is a prominent member of the Committee for the Defense of the Unjustly Persecuted (VONS). Author of numerous political tracts and editor of the *samizdat* periodical *Čtverec*, Dienstbier was arrested in May 1979 and tried in October. He was charged with subversion, sentenced to three years in prison, and refused release despite ill health. Freed in May 1982 and offered the chance to emigrate, he refused. He has recently worked as a stoker and has been detained briefly on several occasions.

Jiří Hájek (1977, 1979) (b. 1913, professor of history and diplomacy, Charles University.) Hájek was ambassador to Great Britain in the 1950s; deputy foreign minister, 1958–1962; head of the Czechoslovak mission to the United Nations, 1962–1965; minister of education and culture, 1965–1968; and minister of foreign affairs under Alexander Dubček. Dismissed from his post in September 1968 on the insistence of the Soviets, he was also expelled from the party in 1970 and forced into early retirement. In 1975 Hájek wrote an open letter to Prime Minister Lubomír Štrougal praising the Helsinki Final Act. Hájek was a founding member of Charter 77 and coauthor of numerous documents, petitions, and appeals. Living under tight police surveillance, he has been warned, detained, and interrogated on several occasions and incarcerated for short periods. He administered the funds to assist the families of persecuted people.

Václav Havel (1977, 1978, 1979) (b. 1936, acclaimed playwright and author whose works are officially banned.) A graduate of the Academy of Dramatic Arts in Prague, Havel spent four and a half months in 1977 in investigative custody following his appointment as Charter 77 spokesman. A prominent VONS member, he was under virtual house arrest from late 1978 until May 1979. Detained in May 1979, Havel was tried in October 1979, charged with subversion, and sentenced to four and a half years in prison. He was transferred to the hospital in February 1983 with serious health problems. Formally released from prison in March 1983, he has periodically been detained since then, including spells in November 1983 and August 1985.

Ladislav Hejdánek (1977, 1978, 1979) (b. 1927, philosopher and mathematician.) After being fired from a post at the Institute of Philosophy at the Academy of Sciences in 1970, Hejdánek could only work as a night watchman and stoker. He spent eight months in prison in 1972 for "attempted instigation." Hejdánek regards himself as a "democratic socialist." A pupil of Professor Jan Patočka, he is coeditor of the literary magazine *Tvář*. He is under constant surveillance, often interrogated, and subjected to detention, physical abuse, and house searches. He jointly administered funds to help families of persectued individuals and conducted unofficial seminars for young people, which were occasionally raided by the police. He recently worked as a stockkeeper.

Marie Hromádková (1980) (b. 1930, historian.) Former

secretary for industry in the CPCS Borough Committee in Prague, she was expelled from the party in 1969 after joining the Information Department of the CPCS Central Committee. Hromádková has since worked as an accountant in a construction firm. She has been arrested for short periods several times since 1977. Her residence was ransacked by the security police in November 1985.

Eva Kantůrková (1985) (b. 1930, writer.) A former youth union official, she renounced her party membership in 1970. After several detentions during the 1970s, she was imprisoned without trial on subversion charges from May 1981 until March 1982. Her book on female activists and wives of prominent dissidents has been translated into several languages, but she is officially barred from publishing in Czechoslovakia.

Jan Kozlík (1983) (b. 1946, electrician and technician.) A graduate of a technical college, Kozlík was expelled from Komenský Theological College in 1971 for political reasons, under pressure from the Ministry of Culture. Since then he has worked as a technical inspector in a Prague construction firm. Detained twice in 1983, he was warned against engaging in activities connected with the World Peace Assembly or with the protest against Soviet missile deployment.

Marie Rut-Křížková (1983) (b. 1936, lecturer in Czech language and journalist.) Rut-Křížková graduated in philosophy from Charles University and was prohibited from working as a journalist after 1968. Following a long unemployed period, she found posts as a forestry worker and in a post office. Her work has been published in *samizdat*. She is a practicing Catholic. Rut-Křížková received a police warning during the World Peace Assembly in June 1983 and was interrogated in November 1983. She is currently employed as a post office clerk.

Marta Kubišová (1977, 1978) (b. 1942, pop singer.) Since 1962, Kubišová has won many competitions and prizes, including the Golden Nightingale Award in 1968/1969. In January 1970, she was prohibited from performing publicly, recording, or traveling abroad, and she now can only obtain manual and secretarial work. Kubišová resigned as spokesperson because of health reasons in November 1978.

Ladislav Lis (1982) (b. 1925, lawyer.) Lis was secretary general of the official Union of Czechoslovak Youth in the 1950s, was persecuted by the regime in the 1960s, and politically rehabilitated during the Prague Spring. Former secretary of the Prague City Committee of the CPCS, Lis was expelled in 1969 and then worked as a forest ranger. A VONS member, he was arrested in 1978, charged with subversion in May 1979, and released later that year. He has been frequently detained since then — three times in 1980 and twice in 1981. He received threats against the lives of his children in 1982. Arrested in January 1983, he was tried in July and sentenced to 14 months in prison. Released in May 1984, he was arrested again the same month and sentenced to three months. In November 1984, Lis was appointed vice president of the International Federation for Human Rights (FIDH). Under constant surveillance since then, he lives on a disability pension.

Father Václav Malý (1981) (b. 1950, ordained Catholic priest.) He worked in the ecclesiastical administration in Vlašim and Plzeň. After state consent for carrying out religious duties was withdrawn in 1979, he worked in a civil engineering firm. A VONS member, he was arrested in May 1979 and released in December 1979. Since 1980 Malý has worked as a stoker. Although arrested several times in 1980 and pressed to emigrate, he refused to leave. Since then, he has been detained for brief periods including in March 1984.

Anna Marvanová (1982, 1983) (b. 1928, journalist.) Marvanová worked for 20 years for Czechoslovak radio in Prague. A party member from 1948 until 1969, she submitted her party card when Dubček was removed from office. She left the radio in 1970 to seek another post, but later had to stop work for health reasons. She is active in protests against police mistreatment of dissidents. In October 1980, "unidentified thugs" attempted to push her under a train in the capital. She was detained in April 1981 but authorities later released her without charge. Although Marvanová suffers from an incurable disease, the regime has threatened to take away her disability pension. She has been detained for brief periods since 1983.

Martin Palouš (1986) (b. 1950, teacher.) The son of 1982 charter spokesman Radim Palouš, Martin Palouš is a graduate in philosophy from Charles University. Upon joining Charter 77 he was dismissed from a teaching post, then worked as a cleaner and stoker until 1980 and is now employed as a computer programmer. Palouš is well known for his essays, which are published mainly in *samizdat*.

Radim Palouš (1982) (b. 1924, doctor of natural sciences and philosophy.) After signing the charter, Palouš was dismissed from Charles University where he worked as an assistant lecturer in chemistry. He is a practicing Catholic and was active in the "Patočka University," which resulted in incarceration in March 1980. Retired because of ill health in 1982, he now lives on a disability pension.

Jan Patočka (1977) (b. 1907, professor of philosophy and Christian activist.) Patočka was dismissed three times from Purkyně University in Brno: by the Nazis in 1939, by the Communists in 1948, and again in 1972 during widescale political purges. He was a founding member of Charter 77. He died of a heart attack in March 1977, after 11 hours of grueling police interrogation.

Bedřich Placák (1981) (b. 1914, professor, surgeon.) Placák was active in Slovak resistance groups during World War II. He was the first Czechoslovak to perform open heart surgery. A CPCS member from 1945 to 1968, he lost his membership for involvement in the Prague Spring and became one of the initial Charter 77 signatories. Placák worked as a clerk and a night watchman in a museum but was dismissed from the museum post in 1981. Passports were withdrawn from his entire family in 1983; he now lives as a pensioner.

Miloš Rejchrt (1980) (b. 1946, ordained clergyman.) Rejchrt was minister of the Protestant Church of Bohemian Brethren and a pastor in Česká Lípa, North Bohemia until deprived of state consent in 1972 to continue religious work. Since then he has worked as a stoker and a maintenance man. Subject to police harassment and intimidation, he was detained in August 1980 for signing a statement of solidarity with Polish workers but was later released.

Jiří Ruml (1984) (b. 1925, journalist.) Ruml worked for *Rudé Právo*, the Communist Party daily, and Czechoslovak radio, became chief editor for political broadcasting in the early 1950s, but was dismissed in 1963 for criticizing the slow pace of de-Stalinization. In 1968, during the Soviet occupation, Ruml was elected delegate to the Extraordinary Party Congress. He was expelled from the CPCS and banned from working as a journalist. After signing Charter 77, he worked as a crane operator and became a VONS member. He has been arrested several times, including imprisonment without trial between May 1981 and March 1982.

Jaroslav Šabata (1978, 1981) (b. 1927, professor of psychology.) A former senior CPCS official and regional party secretary in Brno in 1968, Šabata was suspended from a teaching position at Purkyně University in Brno in 1969 and expelled from the CPCS in 1971. Employed as a construction worker, Šabata was arrested in 1972 for "instigating antistate actions by students" and sentenced to six and a half years in prison. Although released in 1976 on three years probation, he was arrested in October 1978 on fabricated charges and served two years and three months of the sentence. Released in December 1980, authorities arrested him again in November 1983 and later released him. He lives on a disability pension and suffers from heart problems.

Anna Šabatová (1986) (b. 1951.) Šabatová is the daughter of former Charter 77 spokesman Jaroslav Šabata and wife of prominent dissident Petr Uhl. Arrested in 1971 with Uhl and 16 other people for belonging to an illegal revolutionary youth group, she was sentenced to three years in prison for subversive activities and was released in December 1973. Šabatová was a founding member of VONS and an early charter signatory. Since 1979 she has been editing and publishing with Uhl the periodical *Informace o Chartě 77* (Information on Charter 77).

Jan Štern (1986) (b. 1924, journalist and author.) Formerly married to Eva Kanturková (Charter spokesperson in 1985) Štern was barred from the official media after the 1968 invasion. After 1970 he worked as a manual laborer and technical official; he has since retired and lives on a pension.

Jana Šternová (1984) (b. 1921, dancer and director.) A former dancer at the National Theater, Šternová directed a theater company in Karlovy Vary. She was expelled from the party in 1969 for expressing opposition to the Warsaw Pact incursion. Šternová was also detained briefly in January 1985. She had worked as a cleaner but now lives as a pensioner.

Petruška Šustrová (1985) (b. 1947.) Šustrová became a member of a group of nonofficial socialist young people (the Movement of Revolutionary Youth) after 1969. Tried in 1971 for antistate activities, Šustrová spent 13 months in jail and has been detained several times since for briefer periods, including in January 1985.

Zdena Tominová (1979) (b. 1941, writer and translator.) Tominová was dismissed from Charles University in 1978 and has been harassed and intimidated by the police. She was attacked by masked assailants in June 1979 and hospitalized with a concussion. Tominová emigrated to Great Britain in September 1980.

* * *

In February 1980, a 15-member "Collective of Charter 77 Spokespeople" was formed to help the three official spokespersons and to supply speedy replacements if spokespersons were arrested. The Collective's membership was increased to 17 in April 1980. In addition to the spokespersons, who sign and authorize charter documents, a "Charter 77 milieu" or "circle of influence" has crystallized over the years. Larger than the inner group of most committed activists, the circle consists of a loose assemblage of people (an informal community) who individually or together undertake various initiatives. In addition to specific interest groups, such as the VONS, there are informal committees that publish *Informace O Chartě 77*; organize debates and seminars on history, sociology, the economy, and many other issues; arrange private exhibitions and theatrical performances of officially banned plays; and initiate other independent activities.

The charter was signed initially by 243 people before it was made public in January 1977. Since then the number of signatories has steadily climbed. The midyear or year-end totals are shown in table 1. Although about a dozen Charter 77 signatories have withdrawn their names, indications show that withdrawal was the result of pressure applied on them by the authorities. Of the approximately 1,200 signatories, roughly 1,000 actually reside in Czechoslovakia, the rest have emigrated to the West. Approximately one-third of the 1,000 actively engage in Charter 77 work on a regular basis.

An occupational profile of the Charter signatories during the past decade reveals that approximately 38 percent are manual or low status white-collar workers.[17] Many of the reform-minded intelligentsia, however, are not allowed to pursue professional careers, and many of them can only obtain manual work. A further breakdown of the statistics shows that about 11 percent of the signatories are notable figures in the world of culture, 11 percent maintain professional positions of various kinds, and more than 10 percent are scholars. The occupations of nearly 16 percent are difficult to identify. All the signatories fall into the occupational groups shown in table 2.

Approximately 25 percent of the charter signatories are female and about 1.5 percent of the total are pensioners. The percentage of young people in Charter 77 from the post-Prague Spring generation has reportedly been climbing steadily over the years. It is difficult to estimate the exact geographic distribution of all the signatories, but one

TABLE 1
Charter 77—Signatory Trend

Year	Number of Signatories	Year	Number of Signatories
1977	831	1983	1138
1978	937	1984	1163
1979	1017	1985	1190
1980	1065	1986	1200
1982	1101		

TABLE 2
Occupational Profile of Signatories

Occupational Status	Percentage of Signatories
Manual and Low-Level White-Collar Workers	38
Figures in the World of Culture	11
Professionals	11
Scholars	10+
Office Workers	2.9
Clergymen	2.8
Students	1.4
Government Employees	1.1
Housewives	1.3
Former Communist Politicians	1.8
Unidentified	16

can safely conclude that the overwhelming majority reside in Prague and its environs, and most of the others are distributed between a few major cities – including Brno, Bratislava, and Plzeň. Generally speaking, rural dwellers have had much less opportunity to sign Charter 77 or engage in charter-sponsored activities than have urban residents.

It would be misleading, however, to measure the strength and impact of Charter 77 by the gradually increasing number of signatories. As the most outspoken activists in their milieus, the signatories rather represent the visible tip of an iceberg of opposition to government policy; the bulk of the iceberg is submerged in Czechoslovak society.

Internal Divisions

Charter 77 combines several political and nonpolitical groups as well as individuals holding wholly independent positions. The charter does not constitute a formal union of these groups, does not publicly represent any one of them, nor has it evolved into a mouthpiece for their views. It has simply provided a platform and an opportunity for action by people who could subordinate their personal opinions and ideological orientations to the larger human rights cause that Charter 77 represents.[18]

When the charter was launched, one of the largest groups to sign was made up of so-called ex-Communists or reform Communists. Initially, they formed about half of the signatories, but over the years their percentage of the total has gradually declined; they now constitute a minority within the movement. Although 150 of the original signatories were reform Communists of various hues, they represented only a small fraction of the 1968 reform campaigners – approximately one-half million members were expelled from the party in 1970 and 1971. Little open support for Charter 77 has been evidenced among the majority of former Communist functionaries, and many ordinary rank-and-file CPCS members have become thoroughly disillusioned by the results of normalization since 1968. Former Communist Party members either concluded that the outcome of the Prague Spring showed that precious little ultimately could be improved in Czechoslovakia, or they simply were not prepared to risk involvement in another democratic reform movement.

Leading ex-Communists who did sign the charter included Zdeněk Mlynář, Jiří Hájek, Milan Hübl, Rudolf Slánský, and Jiří Dienstbier. They did not form a coherent political group, however, and lacked a common, binding program. In addition, disagreements about strategy surfaced periodically. A section of about 50 former CPCS members, led by Mlynář, were nicknamed the "Tuesdayites," because they always held their meetings on Tuesdays, or the "E-Club," because of their sympathies for Eurocommunism. After the emigration of Mlynář early in 1977, the group practically disintegrated. Various smaller factions emerged but were unable to agree on a joint program. Although the ex-Communists generally were able to subsume their political views and ambitions within the confines of Charter 77, they came under increasing criticism from some younger activists. Many young activists had few, if any, recollections of the Prague Spring and viewed the Communist reformers with suspicion, tending to associate them with the prevailing power structure.

The influence of the reform Communists probably has been most noticeable in the charter's repeated calls for dialogue with the government, in the purposeful avoidance of any conflict, and in the underlying belief that the Communist Party is still capable of reform. At all costs, the reform Communists intended to prevent Charter 77 from developing into a political organization or an overt opposition movement challenging the regime. This resolve was supported by the majority of signatories, who viewed the campaign for civil liberties as a more practical vehicle, given current political conditions, for evincing social and economic improvements.

A second sizable group within Charter 77 is made up of

a mixture of "democratic socialists" and "independent liberals," including such notable figures as Rudolf Battěk. A number of them periodically criticized the ex-Communists for what was perceived as unnecessary moderation and urged more direct political action. Some of them even suggested the creation of an avowedly political organization. Although many of the independent liberals envisaged little prospect for systemic political reforms, they conceded that, given the political impasse, only the application of consistent pressure on the authorities could possibly bring dividends. A campaign for respect for human rights seemed to offer the most realistic chance for success. The independent liberals considered it essential that citizens not passively await internal changes but actively undertake various initiatives themselves. They reasoned that these activities eventually could evolve into a substantial opposition force as conditions became more favorable.

The independent liberals appear to have been the most ardent supporters of the development of parallel structures and various autonomous initiatives such as VONS. They also urged the establishment of working committees for free labor unions and fully supported the pursuit of various international contacts.

A much smaller segment of charter "independents" has consisted of self-styled revolutionary Marxists, led largely by Petr Uhl. They wanted the movement to assume a more radical political stance—for example, by concentrating on agitation work among workers and young people and by openly declaring a revolutionary program of action. The revolutionary Marxists have gained little support among the signatories or among society at large. Uhl, however, was able to subordinate his political views to the broader interests of Charter 77 and won respect from other dissidents for his stamina and organizational abilities.

The third significant element within Charter 77 consists of religious activists who possess links with unofficial religious circles. The role and influence of religious activists in Charter 77 has increased steadily during the last 10 years. The charter provided a forum that helped Protestants, Catholics, and other Christian and non-Christian faiths unite around the campaign for freedom of belief, worship, and assembly. The religious groups have not adopted any specific political orientation, but instead have espoused a practical Christian humanism that enables them to act in concert with the nonreligious chartists. Although Charter 77 continued successfully to resist both internal and external pressures to become more political, a growing number of practicing Christians joined the movement or provided support. Their influence is evident in the charter's avoidance of political activism and its overriding stress on morality, ethics, and freedom of thought and action. Many of the religious chartists are also involved in the "underground church" and help to compile information on official repression of clergymen and believers.

In addition to the more well-defined groups and points of view, Charter 77 has attracted an assortment of independent-minded and unaffiliated intellectuals such as Václav Havel, young people from the "cultural underground," and ordinary citizens without any strong political views but sharing a concern for human rights and social justice. The wide spectrum of orientations within Charter 77 apparently has not included any explicitly nationalist or overtly anti-Communist elements. Splinter groups have not materialized, and a general unity of purpose has been maintained throughout the decade.

From Charter 77's inception, an informal agreement established that the three official spokespersons, who sign and authorize documents, would be chosen from the three main groups — the reform Communists, the Christians, and the independent liberals and intellectuals. This arrangement initially was maintained, but in recent years the independent socialists have predominated among the spokepersons. This may be less a reflection of any growing left wing influence within the charter than an indication that ideological distinctions play no important role in the inner core of Charter 77; the policies and programs of the movement have not been radically altered during its 10-year history.

Nevertheless, internal differences continue to surface occasionally, primarily on the question of campaign priorities — such as the charter's attitudes toward the Western peace movements. Some signatories have been more critical than others of drawing Charter 77 into international political controversies outside the framework of the human rights agenda. Such internal conflicts usually are resolved by allowing scope for many divergent views in charter dossiers and essays. This policy not only has prevented the appearance of serious splits but has also helped stimulate often lively debate within the democratic opposition on numerous pressing issues.

Breadth of Support

Despite its achievements, Charter 77 has been unable to kindle widespread and active support among the majority of the population. A number of interrelated factors hinder independent movements in Communist states from obtaining large-scale support, except under special circumstances.

The nationwide disillusionment that accompanied the 1968 Warsaw Pact invasion, the subsequent crushing of the Prague Spring democratic reform movement, and nearly two decades of paralyzing normalization have left the bulk of society in a resigned mood. Although the overwhelming majority of people are latently hostile to the regime, they visualize little possibility for improvement or for citizens to exert real influence on government policies. Events in Poland since December 1981 have reinforced this viewpoint. Any official moves are observed with enormous suspicion, because the public is mistrustful and cynical about government motives — including Prague's ratification of the UN human rights covenants and other international agreements. Czechoslovak citizens in general remain deeply skeptical about the effectiveness or advisability of any form of independent action, whether explicitly political or principally human rights related. Most people clearly are discouraged by what they perceive as a wide discrepancy between the costs of campaigning for civil liberties and the limited benefits received from any resulting government measures.

A second factor, that severely restricts popular support for Charter 77 and is deliberately cultivated by the regime, revolves around the unwritten social contract between government and society. In return for noninvolvement in unofficial activities and passive acceptance of the internal and international status quo, citizens have been assured an acceptable standard of living with the prospect of modest advancement gained primarily through the officially tolerated "second economy." This system of control worked reasonably well during the 1970s, but now is showing signs of strain because the economic reforms necessary to increase productivity have not been introduced. Although the social contract now stands on shakier ground, it is unlikely to collapse in the foreseeable future, because material conditions are still far from desperate.

Powerful socioeconomic pressures and sociopsychological factors that make people fearful of political involvement continue to operate in Czechoslovak society. Autonomous activities are widely perceived as counterproductive, because they could result in more severe across-the-board repressions and ultimately threaten living standards. A section of the population even seems to resent Charter 77 for posing a menace to the relative tranquility, however much they may ultimately support its aims. In addition, many ordinary citizens view with suspicion any movement that involves former Communist officials, making little distinction between the variants of socialism. As a result, the majority of the population remains passive and avoids involvement in unofficial activities even if they sympathize with the principles and objectives.

A third set of factors that restrict popular involvement in Charter 77 stems directly from the nature of totalitarian communism. The virtually all-pervasive system of controls exerted by the party apparatus is combined with an assortment of administrative and judicial measures, an enormous network of informers, and direct police and security service repression to insure that an individual is disinclined to step out of line. Consequently, the chartists have tended to be isolated from the working class masses and have had enormous difficulty distributing charter materials or finding contact points within the populace. Some also argue that Charter 77 texts rarely appeal to the average citizen; in the early stages, in particular, texts were aimed primarily at intellectuals, government officials, and international agencies and were often written in legalistic language largely incomprehensible to ordinary workers. Nevertheless, many of the points raised by charter documents eventually filter through to the population, though often indirectly – for example, through the broadcasts of Western radio stations beaming Czech or Slovak language programs into the country.

In addition to an absence of open popular support, the charter initiative has failed to attract significant numbers of people from certain sectors of society – such as most of the former CPCS members ousted after 1969, disaffected groups within the party itself, and the majority of religious believers, workers, farmers, and students. The charter's impact in Slovakia has been particularly weak, largely because of the region's isolation from the urban centers of opposition. Another factor is the partial though closely supervised satisfaction of Slovak national aspiration through the official granting of some regional administrative autonomy in education, culture, and the economy. Slovakia was far less affected by the Prague Spring, the Soviet invasion, and subsequent purges than either Bohemia or Moravia, and reformist trends traditionally have been less evident. Some members of the Hungarian minority in Slovakia have displayed an interest in the charter's work, because they are concerned with official discrimination in education, employment, and culture. The Committee for the Legal Protection of the Hungarian Nationality in Czechoslovakia was formed in 1978 and established contacts with some chartists. For its part, Charter 77 has often reported on the problems faced by the Hungarian, Romany, and other national minorities that stem largely from government policies.

On the credit side, Charter 77 has also increasingly gained the patronage of a portion of the younger generation. It is estimated that by 1981 approximately 40 percent of Charter 77 signatories and other active supporters were young people (under 30 years), and the proportion has grown steadily since. An unseen and uncounted patronage includes many individuals who engage in charter work but prefer to withhold their names from publication for fear of reprisals. Experts in various fields, who may be outside the dissident community, supply a substantial amount of materials used to compile charter documents. Many ordinary citizens support the campaign in practical but less visible ways: collecting and supplying information, distributing texts, preparing and typing documents, soliciting signatures, and participating in the multifaceted program of unofficial cultural and educational pursuits.

To calculate the precise number of active Charter 77 and VONS supporters is difficult. Even more problematic is assessing the extent of passive or potential support. No matter how many thousands are involved in human rights activities or in other charter-related endeavors, the numbers have proved sufficient to enable the charter's active minority to persevere despite government persecution. Whatever the actual breadth of support, Charter 77 has clearly contributed to heightening society's awareness about the nature of the political system. It has also helped to incubate the country's democratic traditions during a particularly difficult period of its history.

4

Achievements and Setbacks

The Early Period

The first few months of Charter 77 activities largely consisted of publicizing the campaign at home and abroad, gaining supporters and new signatories for the declaration, and attempting to draw the authorities into fruitful discussion. The immediate reaction of the government to the appearance of Charter 77 was more severe than anyone had anticipated; the movement's founders believed that Prague would pay more attention to world opinion. The regime seemed to be surprised by the charter and by the number of people involved in its preparation. Probably fearing that the campaign could spread rapidly if immediate remedial action was not taken, the government launched a sweeping crackdown against the known signatories and other suspected participants.

During the early weeks of 1977, hundreds of individuals with supposed dissident connections were detained, interrogated, demoted, sacked from work, or suffered other varieties of persecution. A massive media campaign was unleashed, heralded by an editorial on January 7, 1977 in *Rudé Právo*, the party's central daily organ. It was clear that key CPCS leaders had orchestrated the repression, because they were apprehensive about the consequences of inaction and angered by the lack of forewarning and adequate preventative measures. According to Gordon Skilling, an authoritative writer on contemporary Czechoslovakia, the party was confident that "the policy of 'normalization' had achieved relative success, and had created a climate unlikely to produce fresh expressions of dissent."[19] The reaction of the regime was therefore both precautionary and aggressive in its attempts to stifle the opposition. Police and security service detachments were strengthened and placed on alert, and the public was exposed to large doses of anti-charter propaganda. As a result, and contrary to official intentions, practically everyone in the country was quickly made aware of the formation of Charter 77. Without such an overreaction on the part of the authorities, the appearance of the charter may have gone largely unnoticed by the majority of citizens.

Publication of the Charter 77 declaration was expressly forbidden by the government. During a lecture at the Political High School of the CPCS Central Committee on February 24, 1977, Minister of the Interior Jaromír Obzina issued a warning that the Charter 77 text is "so sophisticated that if it were published, 90% of the population would not understand how dangerous it is, and about two million would be prepared to sign it immediately."[20] The government campaign did not run as smoothly as officials had calculated. Assemblies of workers, organized by party activists and encouraged to vote for anti-charter resolutions, often demanded to read the text they were urged to condemn; not surprisingly, the texts were not revealed and workers refused to support the anti-Charter 77 resolutions. As a result, CPCS and labor union officials were required to sign on behalf of employees. The offensive in factories and in the mass media was discontinued when these negative consequences became apparent. From then on, the authorities adopted more sophisticated methods for dealing with the charter.

Despite police harassment and intimidation the chartists did not abandon their campaign. They soon issued further documents, which already numbered 10 by May 1977, and several appeals and open letters. Professor Jan Patočka, one of the three initial Charter 77 spokespersons and a leading force behind the creation of the group, asserted shortly before his death in March 1977, that

> Submissiveness never led to any improvement but only to a deterioration of the situation. The greater the fear and servility, the more daring those in power will become. There is no means by which their pressure can be diminished except by making them insecure, by showing them that injustice and discrimination are not forgotten. That does not imply an exhortation to ineffectual threats, but rather to behavior that is dignified, fearless, and truthful, impressive simply by the manner in which it responds to official behavior.[21]

The chartists defended their objectives and their legitimacy despite the government campaign and soon attracted fresh signatories. The signing of anti-charter statements by labor unions and cultural organizations, under strong pressure from the party *aktiv*, the party's political agitators, did not achieve the desired results; it simply served to increase popular hostility toward the regime. From the outset the prime objective of Charter 77 clearly was not the collection of signatures, but the involvement of wide sectors of society in human rights issues. The charter was intended to awaken the public's conscience by making people aware of the liberties they had been guaranteed in a variety of domestic laws and international agreements and informing them of how these liberties were systematically violated by the Czechoslovak authorities. The founders of the movement hoped that this knowledge, coupled with the example set by the charter signatories, would stimulate popular interest and increase demands for civil rights in various domaines of life.

The birth of Charter 77 marked an important juncture in relations between rulers and ruled in Czechoslovakia.

First, it finally ended any lingering illusions that the Communist government would voluntarily relax the dead weight of normalization. Second, a few hundred courageous individuals had taken an important first step on behalf of the oppressed nation and thereby hoped to encourage others to contribute according to their means and capabilities. During the next decade Charter 77 would experience both setbacks and achievements in its campaign for the official observance of human and civil rights, but would not retreat in scope or substance.

Landmarks and Phases

To examine the most significant events and developments of the past decade it is helpful to divide the history of Charter 77 into a number of phases. The formative period between the winter of 1976 and the summer of 1977 was characterized by a gradual process of consolidation. Early differences between the various strands of the Czechoslovak opposition movement were largely resolved by the close of 1976 with the appearance of the charter-founding declaration. Although most signatories doubted that the authorities would agree to a dialogue, they felt the time was right for such an initiative in the light of domestic and international conditions.

The regime's initial hysterical reaction helped to broadcast widely the existence of the human rights campaign and, ironically, contributed to establishing its credibility in the eyes of the public. Although the authorities failed to strangle the charter at birth, they proved successful in isolating it from the masses. As soon as the government's early propaganda barrage subsided, debate among the leading signatories arose again. By mid-1977, internal discussion on aims and methods, involving more than 200 activists and supporters, revealed some significant differences of opinion. Some of these people thought Charter 77 had already attained its objective and should disband, particularly because prospects for negotiations with Prague looked bleak. Others believed that the chartists should forge a more structured organization with clear-cut political programs and goals. A third position, held by the majority of signatories, upheld the original methods and aims and vehemently opposed any politicization of the movement. A working compromise was achieved by September 21, 1977, when an important new communiqué gave the green light for continuing with current initiatives and expanding their scope wherever possible.

From the fall of 1977 until May 1979, Charter 77 underwent a protracted period of expansion and diversification, despite persistent repression and occasional internal disputes. In many respects, the chartists reached a high point in several initiatives. The principal aims were concerned with accurately chronicling human rights abuses, producing vital documents, reiterating and publicizing the charter's standpoint on various domestic issues, and appealing repeatedly to the government to abide by its own laws. In addition, a number of informal working groups were formed to concentrate on such issues as ecology, free labor unionism, and Charter 77's cooperation with human rights campaigns elsewhere in the Soviet bloc. During this period, VONS was formed to monitor and document specific cases of political persecution and imprisonment. In the international arena, Charter 77 established contacts with the Social Self-Defense Committee-Workers' Defense Committee (KSS-KOR) in Poland and received substantial publicity and support in the West; independent Czechoslovak voices were heard with increasing frequency at a number of international forums.

Charter 77 also helped to invigorate the embryonic "alternative culture," which included the unofficial Patočka University, private concerts, exhibitions, theatrical performances, and the large-scale production of *samizdat* material. By early 1979, substantial progress had been made in raising public awareness about human rights issues, while some damage was inflicted on the regime's image abroad.

Between 1977 and 1979, more than 70 people were sentenced to prison terms for activities related to VONS and Charter 77, but the repression had not yet assumed the extensive proportions of later years. The unofficial movement was not seriously depleted of activists, particularly because a growing number of young people were willing to join its ranks. Nevertheless, through a combination of threats, surveillance, and persecution, police operations prevented the campaign from spreading from the intellectual dissident community into the masses.

Between May 1979 and early 1982, Charter 77 experienced an intensive phase of official repression during which it displayed remarkable resilience. The arrest of 10 VONS members in May 1979 heralded a comprehensive government drive to silence the country's dissidents. The trials in October 1979, in which six prominent oppositionists received long prison terms, failed to silence either Charter 77 or VONS, but did inflict serious damage on the two groups. The authorities ignored the subsequent international outcry and proceeded to detain many chartists for 48-hour periods; an assortment of other pressures were applied more frequently. In the autumn of 1979, a special drive was launched against nonconformist priests, lay Christians, participants in private study groups, and young people involved in the "musical underground." Throughout 1980, the campaign against Charter 77 involved the arrest and long detention of spokesman Rudolf Battěk, police raids on the homes of numerous signatories, and incessant pressure on people either to cease their dissident work or emigrate. Temporary lulls in the crackdown were broken by sudden wide-scale security operations. For example, during May 1981, a series of arrests took in 26 prominent activists, 14 of whom were detained and charged with subversion.[22]

In December 1981, within hours of the imposition of martial law in Poland, a police roundup netted several leading chartists, including spokesmen Václav Malý, Bedřich Placák, and Jaroslav Šabata, who were detained without formal charges. Throughout 1981, the Czechoslovak authorities feared the spread of the Polish democratic disease ("counterrevolution") across the border. They endeavored to prevent contacts from developing between Czech human rights campaigners and Polish Solidarity activists and advisers. After General Wojciech Jaruzelski's coup, the authorities acted swiftly to forestall any domestic expression of support for the Polish free labor union. While world attention focused on Poland and Czechoslovakia disappeared from the limelight, the Prague regime sensed it had a freer hand to strike against its own internal opponents.

Despite the fact that during 1981 the human rights movement suffered its harshest repression to date and lost a number of its activists through imprisonment, intimidation, and emigration, the government's attempt to liquidate Charter 77 fell short of expectations. Charter 77 continued to function because new volunteers readily replaced lost activists. In the words of charter spokespersons in early January 1982,

> Although Charter 77's five years have been five years of persecution and harassment of those supporting it, the activity has not been confined to countering these attacks. The main work continues to lie in constructive attitudes. . . . Charter 77 lives on — because our society still needs it, because the problems pointed to at its initiation are not yet solved, and the attempts to destroy it merely underline the need for its existence.[23]

The years 1982 and 1983 proved to be comparatively subdued in terms of police repression. According to the London-based Palach Press, which is directed by Czechoslovak émigrés and closely monitors events in Czechoslovakia, 1982 marked a quiet period in the official campaign against well-known dissidents.[24] The authorities evidently felt that they could afford to ease the pressure, partly because the immediate danger of a spill-over effect from Poland had subsided — especially after strict travel restrictions between the two states became firmly enforced. Prague also seemed anxious to present a more liberal self-image to the West for political and economic reasons. Seven leading incarcerated activists were released during this phase, and a major political trial, scheduled for early in 1982, was eventually cancelled. Such relaxations notwithstanding, the persecution of lesser-known civil rights supporters continued. Public show trials were no longer staged; instead there was a rise in anonymous threats and assaults against dissidents, in combination with perpetual police harassment. Several oppositionists were tried as ordinary criminals on fabricated charges: Ivan Jirous, prominent in the cultural underground, Jan Wunsch, active in the newly-formed Revolutionary Action Group (SRA), and Jiří Gruntorad, editor of the *samizdat* publication *Popelnice.*

Since 1982 the chartists have increasingly concentrated on what they consider to be the most pressing contemporary issues. Charter documents focused on specific problem areas in social and economic life. Letters, protests, and appeals were issued about the suppression of Solidarity in Poland, calls were made for the withdrawal of Soviet troops from Czechoslovakia, and several supportive messages were sent to peace groups in Western and Eastern Europe. Throughout 1983, with an upcoming Communist Party-sponsored world peace assembly set for June in Prague, Charter 77 focused its efforts on cultivating contacts with nuclear disarmament groups in the West. This dialogue was developed further during 1984 and 1985, despite the problems of communicating through the police dragnet. Many chartists were determined to clarify their views on the closely linked issues of peace and human rights.

As expected, Charter 77 was refused admission to the Prague peace assembly; in response, a letter was drafted by all the available current and former spokespersons and sent to conference participants. Several individuals consequently were detained and threatened by the security services, and the police broke up an unofficial meeting in Prague between several chartists and a group of Western peace campaigners. Also, Ladislav Lis, a leading proponent of contacts between the Czech opposition and Western peace groups, was tried and sentenced to 14 months in prison.

Since 1983 the authorities have faced a grave dilemma — how to prevent Charter 77 from gaining publicity and vigor through ties with Western peace movements while propagating the government's own image as a defender of peace and nuclear disarmament. This may explain why repression of prominent human rights campaigners in recent years has often been moderated largely for foreign consumption.

Throughout the 1980s, and especially since 1983, Charter 77 progressed from being primarily a movement for monitoring the violation of civil liberties into a viable critic of the regime's political, economic, social, and cultural policies. This is evident in a range of documents analyzing urgent domestic problems and in the involvement of a wide circle of sympathizers willing to write authoritatively on such issues.[25] Charter 77 has called repeatedly for extensive debate on the state of the economy and has tried to involve the government in such discussion with little evident success. A degree of moderation has also been noticeable in charter statements since 1984, possibly to avoid unduly provoking the regime and to encourage the release of any remaining political prisoners. Meanwhile, government repression followed the pattern set in preceding years; only one renowned charter signatory, Rudolf Battěk, reportedly remained in prison at the close of 1984. Civil rights activists, however, particularly the lesser-known ones, continued to experience various forms of persecution. Also, a growing number of practicing Christians, especially Catholics, has been hounded by the security forces in recent years, and the same holds true for youths active in the cultural underground.

In July 1985, on the tenth anniversary of the signing of the Helsinki Final Act — a significant landmark for Charter 77 — the chartists released a salient document. They reaffirmed their resolve to persist in their campaign and reminded the Prague government of "its solemn duty to implement the principles and undertakings accepted when our state signed the Final Act."[26] More than a decade after the Helsinki accords, the Czechoslovak authorities still conceded little on the human rights front, while Charter 77 continued to apply pressure at several strategic points.

Activities and Initiatives

The backbone of Charter 77 activities has consisted of compiling, producing, and distributing various texts. These have included numbered documents and statements authorized and signed by the spokespersons, communiqués, letters, individual political or literary essays (*feuilletons*), analytical materials, and current situation reports. They help to explain various charter initiatives and the government's policies as well as to outline concrete proposals for economic and political reform. They are intended for both domestic and international audiences by highlighting conditions in Czechoslovakia and canvasing support for the human rights campaign. The publication of Charter 77 texts is often a complex procedure, because the approval of all available spokespersons is required prior to their release, while police operations obstruct and delay the process. Signed documents represent the widest possible consensus among charter signatories. Controversial documents and analyses, about which there is some internal disagreement, are presented to stimulate a discussion in which responses and counter arguments are welcomed.

Charter documents provide valuable information on conditions within the country about which the regime remains largely silent or distorts the truth. Hundreds of texts have been issued since 1977; the majority are available in the *samizdat* monthly, *Informace O Chartě 77*, which was launched in January 1978.[27] Numerous other unofficial journals have appeared in recent years, some of them only occasionally. In addition, certain economists, historians, and other specialists who sympathize with the charter occasionally release papers or collections of essays on important but officially neglected issues.[28]

The activities of Charter 77 have not been limited to issuing documents, collecting signatures, or presenting letters and appeals to the regime and to international organizations. Many chartists have turned their attention to literature, scholarship, and the arts with a view to developing autonomous educational and cultural programs. The objective is to create a viable second culture with its own parallel structures, separate from the government-controlled bodies. Czechoslovak cultural traditions thereby could be preserved, with only lip service paid to the party-directed institutions. Although no substantial parallel community has yet emerged, independent educational and cultural activities have registered some success, particularly those run for or by intellectuals who were denied professional careers because of their nonconformist opinions and whose works were banned because they conflicted with the dominant ideology. Unofficial Czechoslovak literature was given a pronounced boost in October 1984, when Jaroslav Seifert, one of the first Charter 77 signatories, was awarded the Nobel prize for literature. Some of Seifert's work has been published only in *samizdat* form.

Following the post-1968 purges, the Prague government was determined to uphold "ideological purity" in education and scientific research. The periodic verification of political views of teachers and university staff was introduced as a permanent feature of "cadre work" in higher education. Each staff member must undergo an annual "comprehensive evaluation of political and academic achievements," which, if unfavorable, could result in demotion or dismissal.[29] Charter 77 has publicized the scope of official discrimination throughout the educational system, which often victimizes the children of reformists and political dissenters. In efforts to rectify this situation the chartists have promoted independent seminar courses and a program of learning for young people excluded from higher education. This initiative was called the Patočka University (after the late Jan Patočka) and consisted of lectures presented in private apartments by academics barred from teaching. In addition, a number of Oxford University scholars were invited from England to deliver pertinent lectures. Several of these classes were disrupted by the police, who detained the participants and deported the visiting academics. Founders of the Patočka University frequently experience harassment by the security forces; for example, the philosopher Julius Tomin has been physically assaulted by hired thugs.

On the eve of the cultural forum meeting, held in Budapest in October and November 1985 to review the implementation of Helsinki Final Act stipulations in the sphere of culture, Charter 77 released a statement condemning the Prague regime for its blatant suppression of national culture.[30] The authors listed the repressive elements of the government's cultural policy, including the manipulation of history, ideological distortion of school curricula, the banning of books, art, and films, restrictions on and persecution of numerous artists and scientists, censorship, and self-censorship:

> The consequences of this policy amount to a frontal and deadly attack on the very spiritual, cultural, and hence also the national identity of Czechoslovak society. . . . In the very heart of Europe a comprehensive attack is being waged by the political power on the spiritual integrity and identity of two nations with long cultural traditions.

To counter the official offensive against the free development of culture and learning, several initiatives have blossomed in the 1980s: private concerts, art exhibitions, poetry readings, and theatrical performances staged in the self-styled living-room theater. Hundreds of scholars deprived of work since 1969 and replaced by less talented party loyalists continue to conduct valuable research in their spare time. They often publish their results in typewritten form or in the prolific unofficial press. "Parallel publishing" encompasses literary and scholarly periodicals, regional papers in major cities, foreign affairs journals, discussion journals, economic and political periodicals, and musical and textual cassette tapes.[31] The Edice Petlice (Padlock Edition) publishing house, launched in 1973, issued more than 200 books before closing down in 1983. Other notable independent publishing ventures that have managed to evade police surveillance are Kvart and Expedition. Dozens of books have also been printed individually, reproduced on typewriters, and sometimes extensively circulated; others have been reprinted by émigré publishing houses and smuggled back into the country.

Authors and artists who were expelled from the party and dismissed from work have a modest outlet through the network of underground publishing and private shows; their work is based on merit and not on ideological criteria. Works written by Czechoslovak exiles in the West are also smuggled into the country, then reprinted and circulated. It is estimated that more than 600 officially prohibited titles appeared between 1970 and 1983. Nevertheless, the print runs are still insufficient to reach the general public, which has no other access to many important literary works. Some recent successes have been recorded in the struggle over culture with the authorities. Arduous efforts by a few determined individuals have pressured the regime to permit the publication of formerly banned works. These results should not be exaggerated, however, because the government usually agrees to a publication or a performance after the intervention of the censor, but many authors refuse to have their texts mutilated by state officials.

As far as the chartists are concerned, their activities during the last decade have contributed to a slow but steady progress in

> restoring legal, political, and cultural confidence among citizens [and] in breaking the "iron curtain on information," not only between East and West, and among individual East European nations, but in particular among social groups, regions, industrial works, and finally among individual citizens. . . . Some prog-

ress has also been achieved in demonstrating in a practical and instructive way that concepts such as truth, conscience, responsibility, loyalty, and honor are not simply hollow words, but values that must be adhered to with persistence.[32]

Parallel to defending human rights and sponsoring independent publishing, educational, and cultural pursuits, Charter 77 has developed into a movement to restore "humanism" in social relations—in everyday social contacts and in dealings between officials and ordinary citizens. Charter 77 stresses ethics, morality, honesty, and individual responsibility; people need not become members of any formal organization or even sign the charter, they simply have to behave in a decent way and help recreate "elementary human values" in a hostile, political setting that favors bribery, dishonesty, corruption, greed, and selfishness.

Some chartists claim that their activities overall have had a positive effect on the government. Whether the authorities attack the movement or ostensibly ignore its existence, Charter 77 documents and analyses are scrutinized carefully by officials who, in some cases, take account of problems that the chartists initially publicized. Several topics highlighted in a document have been discussed by the authorities and a partial solution advanced, or the charter thesis is countered, but officials are careful not to publicly reveal whose initiative they are responding to. Pertinent social or economic problems are not, however, subsequently effectively tackled, but the regime feels it is occasionally important to answer certain charges even if only in a roundabout way. The chartists maintain that some sections of the administration are well aware of the "embryonic, independent, checking capacity from below," whose influence could expand in the future.

On several occasions, Charter 77 has advanced concrete proposals for improving relations between government and governed. In a letter to President Husák and Prime Minister Štrougal on April 26, 1985, charter spokespersons expressed concern for the prevailing "social climate."[33] They bemoaned the fact that citizens felt threatened by the "senseless bureaucratization of economic management," the lack of security in work and in their children's future, and by the commonplace hypocrisy, fear, bullying, and helplessness. "The unending stream of young people escaping from the country is the most eloquent testimony to this sense of not really having a home."[34] The chartists suggested that conditions could be improved without disrupting the political system if initiative and dedication were encouraged and if party members were no longer allowed preferential treatment in employment and in the provision of goods, services, and health care benefits.

The document proposes five measures that could ameliorate the situation and regenerate the system of government by making it more productive, dynamic, and flexible. The document recommends

- the lifting of political constraints on hiring and promotion so that people are judged by their abilities;
- the return of individuals who were purged in the past to their appropriate positions;
- the acquiescence to the influence of "Christian and other humanitarian ideas" to improve the moral climate;
- a removal of the ban on the publication of unofficial literature, art, and scholarship;
- the exercise of power subject to "public control";
- a greater role for public opinion;
- a general amnesty to mark the fortieth anniversary of the end of World War II.

By issuing statements on domestic problems and proposing workable improvements or alternative policies, Charter 77 increasingly has assumed the role of an unofficial spokesman for Czechoslovak society in the absence of a democratic system of decision making.

5

Issues and Developments

Related Campaigns

Charter 77 has stimulated and nurtured the formation of other unofficial groups that have set specific aims. The most well known and active of these is VONS – established on April 24, 1978.[35] VONS was inspired by chartists who perceived the need for effective assistance to the victims of repression and their families. Its major objective is to chronicle the case histories of people facing judicial prosecution, imprisonment, or other forms of repression for their independent activities. VONS maintains detailed records of individual cases of persecution, which it makes available to citizens and foreign organizations, including Amnesty International. The committee provides a lifeline, which the authorities have done their utmost to sever, among prisoners, their families, and the outside world. Since May 1978, VONS has regularly issued its own communiqués, documents, and extensive lists of prisoners of conscience.

In December 1978, VONS became a member of the Paris-based International Federation for Human Rights (FIDH) – an associated member of the United Nations. VONS subsequently adopted the subtitle The Czechoslovak League for Human Rights. In November 1984, chartist Ladislav Lis was elected vice president of the FIDH, a member of the FIDH International Bureau, and a permanent federation representative at the United Nations in Vienna. From its inception until mid-1986, VONS has prepared and released over 500 communiqués, statements, appeals, letters, and reports on specific cases of repression. Nevertheless, the committee concedes that it obtains the necessary documentation on only a fraction of actual cases because the authorities make it exceedingly difficult to gather accurate information.

The government treats VONS as an illegal organization, devoid of any international mandate. Numerous VONS members, including many prominent chartists, have been charged with subversion or criminal offenses at various junctures. The arrest of 10 leading VONS activists in May 1979 failed to thwart the campaign, because they were quickly replaced by 12 new members. The trial and conviction in October 1979 of six of them, including Petr Uhl, Václav Havel, Václav Benda, Jiří Dienstbier, and Otka Bednářová, provoked considerable adverse international publicity for the regime. Expressions of support also emanated from many sources inside the country, including people who, until then, had passively observed the human rights campaign. For example, one protest petition was signed by 774 people, of whom nearly 60 percent were not Charter 77 signatories. Regardless of the outcry, Petr Uhl, the last prisoner from the 1979 VONS trial, was not released until May 1984. Despite incessant persecution, the committee continues to issue relevant documents regularly and to underline its solidarity with repressed civil rights activists in other Communist states.

The Preparatory Committee of Free Labor Unions in Czechoslovakia was founded in June 1981. Inspired by events in Poland and by domestic human rights activism, it declared itself "a group which strives for the democratization of the trade union movement."[36] Although it expressed full support for the independent Solidarity union in Poland, the preparatory committee stressed that during the immediate future, it intended to operate within the party-controlled Revolutionary Trade Union Movement (ROH).

The preparatory committee set itself the awesome task of transforming the Communist labor unions so they would properly defend the rights and interests of workers and also "participate significantly in the control and direction of production, and of the economic, social and cultural life of our country."[37] If all legal measures failed, however, the preparatory committee asserted it would launch "a parallel independent trade union movement." The Preparatory Committee of Free Labor Unions in Czechoslovakia has remained anonymous and largely obscure apart from its occasional statements. Its achievements within the official union structures seem negligible thus far, but the group claimed in November 1981 that

> in many factories and in some organizations there are many informal, spontaneously created groups which critically monitor the work of the unions. . . . Only under more advantageous conditions will it be possible to institutionally unite them. We want to help, both directly and indirectly, all these informal groups and individuals who are striving for the renaissance of the trade union movement in Czechoslovakia.[38]

It is difficult to assess the links between the preparatory committee and Charter 77; by withholding the identity of its members, this clandestine group evidently has tried to distance itself from charter signatories and strategies. The group has expressed "high respect" for Charter 77, because "the fate of their signatories and their consistent persecution serves as a warning to us."[39] Only time will reveal the size of the Czechoslovak free labor union movement and the actual extent of its influence among workers. In light of singularly unfavorable political conditions and widespread indifference and cynicism among the working class, immediate prospects for the establishment of autonomous labor organizations look decidedly bleak.

A small, clandestine organization calling itself the Revolutionary Action Group (SRA) was formed in Prague in late 1981. The imposition of martial law in Poland purportedly provided the spark for its creation. The SRA's first public statement appeared only two days after General Jaruzelski's coup. In leaflet form and circulated in several local schools and factories, it declared strong support for Solidarity and called on all Czechs and Slovaks to raise their voices in defense of Polish workers by staging protest actions. The SRA considered the attack on Solidarity "a blow for the entire working class, and above all to the workers in the countries of so-called 'real socialism'." It warned the public that if the Polish "renewal process" is crushed "at its inception, you will also feel the consequences, which will include the worsening of the international situation resulting from the ending of the process of relaxation."[40]

Although the SRA scored little success in stirring the population out of resignation and apathy, the government response indicated that it treated the group's efforts seriously. During January and February 1982, the police detained and interrogated several individuals allegedly associated with the SRA. A trial eventually was held in December 1982, at which three workers and a clerk were sentenced to four years in prison. They were charged with subversive activities, consisting of duplicating and distributing printed material published by Czechoslovak émigrés and by Poland's Solidarity, which "slandered the leading role of the Communist Party, the socialist character of the Republic, and its relations with other socialist countries, especially with Poland." One of the defendants, Václav Soukup, was accused of trying to "contribute to the importation of the Polish crisis situation into Czechoslovakia." Another prisoner, Jan Wunsch, was assailed by the prosecutor for founding an organization – the Independent Group for Press and Information – and attempting to use it to subvert young workers and high school students. Wunsch refused to testify and did not confess to any of the allegations.

An SRA statement released in April 1982 asserted that

they benefited from "the full support of the Czech opposition movement" as well as from "significant support among the working people, particularly in the industrial areas of Central Bohemia."[41] Such claims cannot be verified, and indeed may be largely wishful thinking. The SRA possesses no formal ties either with Charter 77 or with VONS, and its relations with the Preparatory Committee of Free Labor Unions in Czechoslovakia are difficult to trace. One can deduce from SRA statements that, from a "revolutionary socialist" perspective it is more explicitly opposed to the Communist regime than are other groups. Although the SRA apparently has made an effort to enlist the support of workers, its current membership is probably small, especially since the 1982 trial, and its influence in the country has seemed insignificant.

The Youth Protest

Throughout the last decade an alternative "youth underground," involving many ordinary young people, has taken root in Czechoslovakia. It is not easy to calculate the percentage of the younger generation actively engaged, but judging by the demand for music, literature, and fashion disapproved of by the regime, the influence of this "counter culture" is considerable. "Alternative" rock-music bands, barred from performing publicly and often hounded by the police for their nonconformist attitudes and unorthodox compositions, form the backbone of this youth movement. Several major personalities in the youth underground have been detained and imprisoned for various periods since the mid-1970s. Among them is the popular poet and art theoretician Ivan Jirous, who has served at least four prison terms and is officially depicted as an "especially dangerous recidivist."

A growing number of young people resent the system for its numerous restrictions on cultural and educational activities and on personal freedom in general. In the absence of clearly formulated political aims, they demonstrate their rebellion against the official straightjacket by composing, performing, and listening to banned or blacklisted music and poetry. Popular protest songs and other rock lyrics with political overtones are reportedly taped, transcribed, typed, and widely circulated in the country.[42] The regime considers much of rock music and the attitudes it engenders among young people to be a serious challenge to its rule, but has been unable to suppress or fully control it since the 1960s. In the late 1970s and throughout the 1980s, Prague has had to contend with the novel phenomenon of punk rock – in many respects more antiauthoritarian and decadent than traditional rock in the eyes of officials, who have correspondingly stepped up their repressive measures. At least 35 "new wave" bands were forbidden to perform in 1983, while formal sponsors, who are necessary to stage all public shows, were intimidated. Numerous dissenting letters have been dispatched complaining about the official anti-rock campaign; even some local branches of the government-sponsored Socialist Youth Union have participated in these protests.

More than 50 notable and popular rock groups continue to exist and attempt to stage occasional performances; punk rockers in particular enjoy a large following. Their music is rebellious, and though Western new wave influence is pronounced, they have created a specific domestic genre, replete with irony, humor, and often biting social comment. One dramatic illustration of official repression of unauthorized rock music and young people's spontaneity occurred on June 11, 1983.[43] A rock festival scheduled for Zabcice, near Brno, was banned by the government at the last moment. The majority of young people arriving at the concert site were unaware of the ban. They then gathered in a Brno park, where the police moved in and arrested several people. The youths shouted slogans about peace and freedom, whereupon police reinforcements arrived and proceeded to attack the youths with truncheons, tear gas, and unmuzzled dogs. Several dozen people were detained, of whom four later received prison sentences. The chartists believe that in its close supervision of such phenomena as creative modern music, the Czechoslovak authorities are probably more repressive than other Communist regimes. The incident in Brno underscores this assessment.

The government has also employed more subtle tactics to control rock music and channel youth discontent in the desired direction. Unable to stifle young peoples' interest in modern music styles and weary of exacerbating their frustrations, officials are evidently intent on sponsoring groups and concerts that do not overtly challenge the principles of the communist system or its ideological underpinnings. Plans are afoot to permit clubs for "young music" to operate within the framework of the Socialist Federation of Youth, and the government allowed Rock Festival '86 to take place in June 1986 at Prague's Palace of Culture, with the participation of about 80 popular rock bands.

One recent conflict between the government and young music followers revolved around the Jazz Section of the Union of Czech Musicians, which was formally banned by the Ministry of Culture in 1984.[44] Despite the prohibition, members of the Jazz Section have become even more active by publishing various material for young people, screening rock music videos, and sponsoring seminars and discussions with musicians. In 1985 they planned to raise funds for the Ethiopian famine victims by producing a tape of Czechoslovak rock bands for public purchase. The regime responded by confiscating proceeds from the sales, evidently outraged that the initiative was undertaken with disregard for official channels.

The crackdown against the Jazz Section continued throughout 1986. Its offices were closed and key members – including the chairman, Karel Srp – were arrested in early September and charged with the illegal publication and distribution of printed material. An ad hoc Committee of Activists of the Jazz Section was promptly formed to protest the government's measures.[45] The committee addressed two open letters – to the CSCE review conference in

Vienna and to the Czechoslovak press agency Ceteka—to publicize its predicament and protest against official repression of independent cultural life.

The party leadership has recently voiced concern about "political apathy" of a large segment of the country's youth, who avoid involvement in official youth organizations and government-sponsored activities.[46] The chairman of the Socialist Youth Union, Jaroslav Jenerál, speaking at the seventeenth CPCS Congress in March 1986, bemoaned the fact that the union had a limited influence among the young. Deputy Prime Minister Ladislav Adamec admitted that young people are "particularly sensitive to society's stagnation and take it badly when they see their country lagging behind world developments."[47] Officials largely attribute the alienation of youths to the weakness of ideological education in schools, the influence of the Western media, and hostile family backgrounds, which are not conducive to inculcating support for the communist system. The authorities seem to be gearing up for more intensive ideological indoctrination in schools to counter "alien influences" among children.

Many young people are becoming increasingly involved in religious education and ceremonies outside school, with active parental encouragement. As much a protest against the regime's militantly atheistic propaganda and its stifling of any ideological dissent as a genuine reflection of growing religious belief, their actions are both an act of defiance and an act of faith. Many youths, also, implicitly or explicitly criticize government policies, and some are associated with the movement for human rights. In certain regions, young people have shown enthusiasm for the campaign for environmental protection. Such initiatives have been reported in the Chomutov area of northern Bohemia, where a group of youths considered it their moral duty to improve the rapidly deteriorating ecology in their region.[48] They contacted a sizable number of friends in the northern and western areas of Bohemia with the intention of forming a citizens organization to campaign against environmental pollution.

The organizers were swiftly rounded up by the police, inter-rogated, and pressured to abandon their initiative. Police intimidation produced the desired effect, and the ecological crusade was nipped in the bud.

Some youths participate in the fledgling independent peace movement by occasionally helping to distribute leaf-lets, such as during the controversy over stationing Soviet nuclear missiles on Czechoslovak territory in the fall of 1983 and in early 1984. During the officially arranged peace assembly in Prague in June 1983, several hundred young people staged an unauthorized "peace and freedom" march in the streets of the capital before the police dispersed them. In December 1985, 295 youths reportedly signed a petition addressed to Gustáv Husák protesting "against the deployment of nuclear missiles in both parts of Europe."

One Charter 77 document has warned the authorities that depriving young people of the music, fashion, and activities of their choice can only lead to feelings of frus-tration, hopelessness, and emptiness, which in turn will "strengthen the latent tensions in society."[49] The regime's policies contribute toward turning young people into "alco-holics, drug addicts, potential political dissidents, or – and this is probably the aim – indifferent conformists." The chartists envisage that

> the energy now suppressed in young people will eventu-ally find an outlet which will be more dangerous to the authorities than all the protest and controversial art, which they are so afraid of that it leads them to ban everything which slightly deviates from their taste.[50]

The Underground Church

Czechoslovakia can claim one of the worst records among Communist states with regard to religious freedoms.[51] The government strictly controls the Roman Catholic church and the various Protestant churches. The church hierarchies particularly must yield to official directives concerning all their activities. In sum, 18 churches and religious communities are legally permitted to function.[52] The authorities have endeavored for nearly four decades, however, to erode their social base and influence and have registered considerable success, particularly in Bohemia and Moravia.

The State Office for Church Affairs oversees and approves the appointment of clerics and can withdraw their licenses to practice without any explanation. It controls the churches' administration and finances, manages church property, regulates religious instruction in schools, supervises church publishing ventures, and strictly controls contacts with religious groups in the West. Individuals employed in education, health, and in numerous other professions are subject to sanctions at work or even dismissal if they openly attend church services or participate in other religious ceremonies. The government-controlled Association of Catholic Clergy, *Pacem in Terris*, which closely monitors the activities of officially approbated priests and involves them in Prague's peace campaigns, was formally proscribed by a Vatican decree in March 1982. The Czechoslovak primate, František Cardinal Tomášek, has been vilified by the regime for condemning *Pacem in Terris* and for allegedly seeking to "destroy socialism" in the country. Because of the government's antireligious policies, there is a general shortage of clerics and religious literature, and educational facilities for religious instruction are clearly inadequate to meet popular demand.

Because of the incessant official pressure on all religious organizations, Charter 77 has received little or no formal support from any of the churches. Nevertheless, a sizable number of clerics and lay workers sympathize with the human rights movement, and some of them actively provide help. During the past decade, the charter has also gained the backing of ordinary religious believers, both Catholic and Protestant, whose influence on the civil liberties campaign has grown accordingly.

Religious observance has been revived in recent years, especially among the young. The regime itself estimates that there are nearly 5 million "active" religious believers (out of a population of more than 15 million) and several million more who do not hold "atheistic attitudes." Officials frequently complain about the number of young people attending church services, particularly in Slovakia. The government has waged a vehement antireligious campaign in both words and deeds, against which Charter 77 has protested numerous times. It is estimated that at least 100 Catholic priests and other clerics were serving prison terms in 1981, and the figure increased during 1983 when police actions against believers multiplied. The repression often takes place in the provinces and therefore receives little publicity in the West.[53] Priests who conduct religious services, provide Bible instruction, or disseminate religious literature without the authorization of relevant state bodies are charged with "obstructing state supervision of Churches and religious societies" under article 178 of the penal code.

Recent years have witnessed the flowering of what has been designated the "underground" or "catacomb church." This description is misleading because no alternative or parallel church structures have been established; on the contrary, the idea is to supplement official church activities by ignoring state directives and operating independently. The chief followers of unofficial religious activity are young people who participate in clandestine religious classes conducted by several hundred priests who have been denied official permits. There is also an interest in monasticism among the young, even though monasteries and convents are officially banned and monastic activity is outlawed. Catholic *samizdat* in Czechoslovakia is probably the most prolific of religious *samizdat* in the Soviet bloc and reportedly enjoys a wider circulation than Charter 77 materials. Publications include books, translations, philosophical tracts, reports on the persecution of believers, and the monthly Czech religious periodical *Informace o Církvi* (Information about the Church).[54]

The election of a Polish and, hence, Slavonic pope in 1978 has energized religious believers in neighboring Czechoslovakia, and not only the Catholic population. In opposition to government policy, Catholics sent a petition to Pope John Paul II, inviting him to visit the country; possibly as many as 30,000 people were said to have appended their names to this document by early 1985. Such a pilgrimage is not likely in the foreseeable future because of Prague's hard-line stance.

Many believers find the current government policy toward the churches grossly oppressive and religious freedoms practically absent. There was a large-scale police operation against priests and believers during September and October 1981. During another severe crackdown in March 1983 against the Franciscan and Dominican orders and various clerics and laymen, some 250 people were taken into custody and interrogated. During house searches conducted in more than a dozen cities, religious literature, money, and typewriters were confiscated.[55] This action sparked off protests, including a letter of complaint to Cardinal Tomášek signed by nearly 4,000 Protestants and Catholics; the first occasion since 1968 that opposition to official policy manifested itself on such a scale. All the detained monks and priests were gradually released from detention during the following months.

Amnesty International regularly reports on cases of religious persecution in Czechoslovakia. According to its data, in July 1984, 10 young Catholics were convicted of "incitement" by the district court in Olomouc and received suspended sentences ranging from 6 to 18 months.[56] Religious activists are often detained and charged under article 178 of the penal code for "offenses" that include teaching religion to children, using their apartments to provide religious instruction, and preparing young people for Holy Communion without official permission.

The religious revival has continued unabated despite a host of legal restrictions on religious life, the incessant detention of priests and laymen, and the harassment of practicing believers. An estimated 150,000 people took part in the Methodius celebrations in Velehrad, southern Moravia, on July 7, 1985, to mark the 1,100th anniversary of the death of St. Methodius; about two-thirds of the attendants were young people. The regime appeared to be surprised by the large turnout and disturbed by how the event evidently strengthened the position of the Catholic church.[57]

Practicing Catholics began to experience greater harassment during the months after the Velehrad commemorations, as tensions between state and church visibly mounted. Forty Catholic activists were arrested in the Gottwaldov region of Moravia in November 1985 and their copying equipment and religious literature confiscated. Since January 1986, the official atheistic campaign has been revitalized in the media.[58] Meanwhile, the number of newly ordained clergymen who have been denied a license to perform their religious duties is said to have reached 400 by May 1986, provoking protest letters to President Husák from aggrieved clerics. Furthermore, reliable estimates indicate that about 100 priests and activists of various denominations have been incarcerated in prisons or psychiatric clinics for several years for engaging in unofficial religious work.[59]

Charter 77's relations with the church hierarchies are likely to remain restricted in the future, largely because of the state's strict supervision of the church. One of the chartists' main postulates is the complete independence of all churches and religious communities from the state, including easy access to religious education for all citizens. Similar demands from a growing number of ordinary people could signify potential problems for the regime in the years ahead.

The Peace Movement

From 1982 onward, Charter 77 energetically promoted its contacts with various nuclear disarmament groups in Western Europe. From the outset it made clear its position on the indivisibility of peace and human rights. The chartists affirmed that a government can mount a genuine campaign for international peace only if it respects human rights at home. By implication, the officially-sponsored peace initiatives in Czechoslovakia (and elsewhere in the Soviet bloc) were fraudulent, because they emanated from a regime that denied basic civil liberties to its citizens and violated all international human rights agreements.

Charter 77 has issued a legion of letters and statements on peace during the past four years. Ladislav Lis has been the principal driving force behind the dialogue with those Western peace movements that were willing to listen to independent voices in Eastern Europe. Although the Charter does not consider itself a peace movement, it maintains that the defense of peace is a legitimate part of the human rights campaign, particularly in the absence of an authentic popular peace movement in Czechoslovakia. The chartists believe that a genuine campaign for peace in both West and East is "an expression of profound civic responsibility," and that dialogue between the various peace groups is "absolutely essential." The chartists have stressed, however, their opposition to unilateral nuclear disarmament and other "unbalanced concessions" by the West. This has led to disagreements with some of the West European peace campaigns. Charter 77 evidently feels most comfortable with Western groups that openly endorse the link between peace in Europe and the restoration of human rights in the Soviet bloc.

Charter spokespersons feel that peace and civil rights should be guarded worldwide by ordinary citizens and unofficial groups who engage in constructive dialogue to influence their respective governments. To promote this view, grassroots East-West dialogue contacts have been established with, among others, the British-based European Nuclear Disarmament (END), the Dutch International Peace Council (IKV), the Danish Nej Til Atomvaben (NTA), and the West Berlin Group for East-West Dialogue. In June 1983, the chartists were refused entry to the World Assembly for Peace and Life Against Nuclear War, which was held in Prague and attended by representatives of official Communist "peace movements," as well as delegates from an assortment of Western nuclear disarmament campaigns. Concurrently, an unofficial meeting in the capital between charter activists and members of several Western peace groups attending the assembly was broken up by the police. Charter 77 signatories were also denied permission to travel to the Third International Conference of European Peace Groups, staged in Perugia, Italy in July 1984. The regime has lucidly underscored that in Communist states the problems of international peace and nuclear disarmament are solely the domain of government officials.

Charter 77 delivered a detailed account of its position on peace and related issues to the Prague peace assembly and enclosed a 200-page collection of documents containing all charter materials on international peace.[60] One of the essays, by former spokesman Jaroslav Šabata, contains an appeal to all unofficial peace movements and human rights groups in the East and West to formulate a "joint long-term political strategy" that would lead to an "abolition of the undemocratic legacy of the post-war social and political settlement, and the unification of Europe." In August 1982 and on subsequent anniversaries of the Soviet invasion, Charter 77 has demanded the withdrawal of Soviet troops from Czechoslovakia, because there was no legal basis for the Soviet presence and their departure would "contribute towards detente in Central Europe."[61] The charter's stance is clearly in line with its emphasis on the inseparability of peace and freedom in the Soviet bloc.

The official announcement in the fall of 1983 that the Soviets would deploy SS-21 and SS-22 nuclear missiles in Czechoslovakia (avowedly to counter the installation of U. S. intermediate-range nuclear weapons in Western Europe) provoked a considerable public outcry in the country. Unconfirmed reports indicated that some kind of unofficial peace movement was emerging, largely separate from Charter 77. Following the Soviet declaration that their weapons were already being installed, antimissile protests were reported in various cities. Protest letters, petitions, and leaflets were circulated in several schools and factories, and a few small-scale public demonstrations took place.

On November 5, 1983, the party daily *Rudé Právo* disclosed that it had received "stacks of letters" opposing Moscow's decision to deploy more missiles on Czechoslovak territory. Evidently most of the readers who objected to the Kremlin's measures were not connected with the Charter, because the authorities would be unlikely to publish dissidents' views. The Prague authorities presumably hoped to release some domestic pressure by showing that society's views were being taken into account. Dissent against Soviet missile installment was registered in several universities, high schools, and work enterprises in Prague and Brno. Despite police raids and the confiscation of documents, one petition alone, dated January 1984, contained nearly 1,000 signatures disapproving of the new weaponry in the Czech lands. A letter from 24 workers in a Hradec Králové factory carried a stinging attack on the missile deployment, together with demands for "the immediate dismantling of all similarly equipped rockets that have been deployed on the territory of our state for some time."[62]

On issues of peace, nuclear disarmament, and the presence of Soviet troops in Czechoslovakia, the government could be faced with more protests in the future. In particular, young people who may not have been involved previously with the human rights campaign could perceive a more immediate cause to channel their dissatisfaction. About 1,000 youths took part in a march in Prague on December 8, 1985, organized to commemorate the fifth anniversary of the death of rock star John Lennon. The organizers read a declaration protesting the stationing of nuclear missiles in both Eastern and Western Europe and collected signatures in support of their initiative. Unlike in previous years, the police did not intervene, despite some of the openly antiregime slogans. The demonstrators dispersed peacefully after a few hours.[63]

The chartists have intensified their "peace campaign" since 1983, a year in which six charter documents focused on peace. They propose that the withdrawal or reduction of Soviet forces in Czechoslovakia should be part of the disbanding of the division of Europe into two blocs and would be an important step toward genuine "peaceful coexistence" on the continent. In a statement of August 19, 1984, Charter 77 asserted that the crushing of the Prague Spring initiated a further escalation of the arms race. The text emphasized that the credibility of Soviet peace proposals was seriously undermined by the 1968 invasion and the continuing presence of Soviet troops. House searches were conducted at the homes of well-known dissidents on the sixteenth anniversary of the Soviet incursion; documents were confiscated and 10 individuals were taken into 48-hour custody and interrogated – including the three charter spokespersons.

In March 1985, the chartists released a major document entitled "The Prague Appeal," which addressed the problems of peace, military disarmament, and international relations.[64] It called for a "reunification of Europe" through meaningful dialogue and East-West cooperation. General propositions were outlined in the document: the creation of nuclear-free zones, increased contacts between states, agreements on the nonuse of force, a rapprochement between COMECON and the EEC, negotiations aimed at the dissolution of the Warsaw Pact and NATO, and the withdrawal of U.S. and Soviet troops from Europe. On the whole, such proposals and remedies seem general and simplistic; indeed, they partially mirror the campaigning slogans of many Western nuclear disarmament groups. These proposals lack substance and realism and, in many respects, play directly into Moscow's hands. A major Kremlin objective is to hasten the removal of U.S. troops and NATO's nuclear weaponry without meaningful corresponding Communist concessions and thus to leave Soviet forces at an easy striking distance, both militarily and politically, from West European capitals.

Notwithstanding some of its more problematic proposals on peace issues, the Charter 77 group has on occasion openly criticized "that section of the peace movement in the West" whose propositions and programs are closely linked to the policies of Warsaw Pact governments.[65] The chartists have also condemned "myopic pacifism which regards the peace movement as nothing more than a movement opposed to weapons, chiefly nuclear ones," thus failing to understand the "circumstances which dictate arms policies." They consider the questions of political democracy, human rights, and civil liberties essential: "the basic values of justice, freedom and human dignity are superior to a mere concern for biological survival."

In an open letter to END and the London-based Campaign for Nuclear Disarmament (CND) in May 1984, Charter 77 stressed its opposition to unreciprocated Western nuclear disarmament, which in the absence of "civilian control over the centers of political and military power [in the Soviet bloc] would sharply increase the threat to the whole of humanity."[66] Charter signatories themselves seem divided on whether to cultivate further contacts with West European peace groups or to stick more closely to domestic civil rights issues. Some individuals have even advocated the formulation of a "new political strategy," spanning East and West and revolving around the peace initiative, to break the status quo of a divided Europe. Throughout this debate the chartists have tried to assure the public that Charter 77 statements on peace and nuclear disarmament represent the widest possible consensus within the movement.

International Dimensions

From its inception, Charter 77 has regarded itself as one ingredient in a worldwide movement to defend human rights and not simply an internal Czechoslovak concern. Chartists therefore have sought contacts, both in the West and East, with similar campaigns or with organizations sharing the political orientations of the charter's component groups. In their foreign contacts, the chartists have deliberately discriminated against the more openly anti-Communist, émigré organizations. Under the influence of "reform Communists," such as Jiří Hájek and Zdeněk Mlynář, the chartists initially welcomed contacts with Communist and Socialist Parties in Western Europe. They soon became disillusioned with the Eurocommunism movement, however, upon discovering that West European Communist Parties generally avoid providing tangible support for human rights groups in the Soviet bloc.

More fruitful links, promoted by the Charter's "democratic socialists," were established with Western Socialist and Social Democratic parties. Declarations of support for Charter 77 have been forthcoming from the Socialist International, and contacts have been developed with various independent West European left wing groups. The Charter's exiled signatories and support organizations in the West often have acted as intermediaries – including the "Charter 77 Club," founded in 1982 as the only organization of charter signatories outside the country. With the club's assistance, press conferences on important events and repression in Czechoslovakia have been held in several European capitals, charter and VONS documents publicized, campaigns mounted demanding the release of political prisoners, and funds gathered to assist the human rights campaign.

Contacts with independent groups in Eastern Europe have proved more difficult to maintain. Nevertheless, Charter 77 did establish useful relations with the Workers Defense Committee (KOR) in Poland. Meetings between members of both groups were held on the Polish-Czechoslovak border in August and September 1978. The sessions produced declarations of solidarity with dissident groups in the USSR, the German Democratic Republic, Hungary, and Romania. The Czechoslovak police prevented a scheduled third meeting from materializing. Despite intensive security service interference in both countries, Charter 77 and

KOR managed to maintain contact through letters, telephone calls, and mutual statements of support. Chartist Jan Tesař, in particular, considered it essential to develop intimate relations with like-minded movements in other communist states; he advocated especially close links with the neighboring Poles and Hungarians. The planned agenda included the creation of working groups to draft joint documents and arrange political seminars. Weary of this form of international solidarity, the regime clamped down to prevent further cross-border cooperation. The success of Poland's Solidarity during 1980 and 1981 increased the Prague government's unease that Polish reformism and free labor unionism could be imitated in Czechoslovakia. As a result, tourism between the two countries was severely curtailed, even after the imposition, suspension, and lifting of martial law in Poland.

Charter 77 and other unofficial groups periodically release statements about the situation in Poland, chiefly to protest against the unremitting repression. Prominent dissidents have also made individual appeals. Playwright Václav Havel addressed an open letter to General Jaruzelski in May 1985, pleading for the release of three leading Solidarity activists on the eve of their trial in Gdansk. A similar letter, written by Ladislav Lis, was dispatched to Jaruzelski in June 1985 on behalf of VONS and the FIDH. A joint appeal was made public simultaneously in Prague and Warsaw on February 12, 1984 by 22 Czechoslovak and 24 Polish human rights campaigners. It called for the "observance of human rights, an extension of civil liberties," and "democracy, sovereignty, and the freedom of our countries." The activists also requested that world public opinion join in efforts to free all political inmates in the two states.

On November 30, 1984, VONS sent an open letter to the independent "citizens committees in defense of legality" in Poland. These committees were established in several cities to monitor police repressions following the murder of Father Jerzy Popieluszko by security service officers. Clearly there was an affinity between VONS and the Polish initiative. Charter 77 reacted with "loathing and outrage" at the death of Popieluszko, condemned all acts of political terrorism, and reaffirmed the common bonds between Poland and Czechoslovakia.[67] As proof of continuing contacts between the Polish opposition and the Charter, the April 1986 edition of *Informace o Chartě 77* carried a four-page interview with Janusz Onyszkiewicz, a former Solidarity spokesman.

A clandestine meeting between Polish and Czechoslovak dissidents was apparently arranged in the first half of June 1986 at an undisclosed location.[68] The participants discussed the possibilities for cooperation on human rights issues, as well as "the liberation of culture from state control" and the prospects for peace based on respect for individual and national rights. Several independent Polish groups have recently offered to cooperate with Charter 77, particularly in the exchange of information and the promotion of joint initiatives. They include the unofficial Polish-Helsinki Committee, which monitors and chronicles human rights abuses in Poland.

Charter 77's contacts with autonomous groups in other Soviet bloc countries have proved even more sporadic, consisting primarily of mutual messages of support to the local dissidents. On March 12, 1984, 19 leading members of the democratic opposition in Hungary addressed a declaration to Czechoslovak and Polish oppositionists emphasizing their backing of Charter 77 and the Solidarity movement. Miklos Duray, a campaigner for the rights of an approximately 600,000-strong Hungarian minority in Slovakia and a victim of official persecution in recent years, added his signature to the charter in early 1984. A number of intellectuals inside Hungary also has condemned the discriminatory policies of the Prague regime; they have been joined by several Slovak activists who sent letters of protest to the government. Duray considers the systematic violation of human rights throughout Czechoslovakia as the primary factor responsible for the mistreatment of the Magyar minority. The mistreatment is not a question of ethnic conflict; hence Duray's support for Charter 77. Contacts with Hungarian dissidents have been strengthened somewhat recently and revolve around two issues: the treatment of the Hungarian minority and the impending ecological problems associated with the proposed Hungarian-Czechoslovak Danube hydroelectric project.

During 1984 the chartists initiated three joint appeals with Polish, Hungarian, and East German dissidents on the question of world peace and human rights. A declaration released on November 22, 1984 entitled "A Joint Statement of the Independent Defenders of Peace in the German Democratic Republic and the Czechoslovak Socialist Republic" was signed by 16 charter signatories and 17 independent East German peace activists. The date marked the first anniversary of the siting of Soviet SS-21 and SS-22 missiles in Czechoslovakia and the GDR. The statement condemned the denial of civil rights wherever they occur and underscored that peace and human rights are two sides of the same coin. The signatories also suggested that limited contacts were being maintained with autonomous peace activists elsewhere in the bloc, including the Soviet Union. The charter's "Peace Appeal" of March 1985, which was addressed to peace movements in both East and West, was endorsed later by 21 leading unofficial activists in the GDR, by the independent "Praxis" group in Yugoslavia, and by the Committee for Social Resistance (KOS) in Poland. Some disagreements were voiced, however, about comments referring to German reunification and the significance of the Helsinki accords.

A joint communiqué, which may prove to be something of a landmark in international dissident solidarity in Eastern Europe, was issued on the thirtieth anniversary of the Hungarian revolution in October 1956. It involved 120 prominent opposition activists from four states – Czechoslovakia, Hungary, East Germany, and Poland – including 24 Charter 77 activists. The signatories declared their

joint determination to struggle for political democracy
in our countries, their independence and democratic in-
tegration, as well as for the rights of all minorities.[69]

Charter 77 has solicited international support by bas-
ing its existence on UN covenants and other international
agreements. The chartists, however, rarely have called directly upon the UN to undertake action on their behalf by
pressuring the Czechoslovak government to observe human
rights codes. Such measures were deliberately avoided in
order to deflect possible charges that Charter 77 was pro-
moting "Western interference" in the country's internal affairs — especially in light of Prague's claim that human
rights were solely a matter for domestic jurisdiction. In addition, the chartists seem to harbor little faith in the effectiveness or willingness of the UN to influence East European regimes. These doubts were confirmed for the chartists
in October 1978, when their letter that explained that appeals to the Communist authorities had elicited no response
was sent to UN Secretary General Kurt Waldheim and all
heads of state who signed the Helsinki Final Act. The letter
was virtually ignored and no action taken. During his visit
to Prague in February 1984, UN Secretary General Javier
Perez de Cuellar was presented with a letter from the Charter 77 group that requested a meeting at which the chartists could tell him about the position of "citizens working
for the consistent application of UN principles in our society." The meeting did not take place, but it remains unclear
whether de Cuellar pressed the government to improve its
human rights record.

The chartists have monitored all international meetings dealing with civil rights, including the Helsinki follow-
up conference in Madrid, which produced the "Concluding
Document" in 1983. A letter to Husák in November 1983,
stated that the provisions of the document regarding human rights "represent an important step forward" and
welcomed the convening of future conferences on these issues. Referring to the Madrid document, the letter appealed

to the Czechoslovak regime to support the creation of an international human rights committee and to protect the domestic civil liberties movement "against acts of arbitrariness on the part of the security forces and other *apparats*."[70]

Charter 77 systematically has enclosed letters and documents to each of the Helsinki follow-up sessions explaining its predicament and Prague's record on the issues under review. In May 1986, the three spokesmen sent a letter to the Bern Conference of Experts of CSCE member states that examined the current state of interpersonal contacts between East and West. They outlined how the Prague authorities hinder contacts between Charter 77 and foreign visitors and impose barriers to restrict links between citizens and their relatives living abroad. The long-term effects of the Helsinki follow-up conferences on civil rights in Czechoslovakia and other Communist states remains to be seen. Although dramatic improvements are not in the cards, at least the human rights sessions will continue to highlight the abuses and provide international recognition and legitimacy for groups such as Charter 77.

Some international agencies have adopted more decisive support for the charter. In 1978 the governing body of the International Labor Organization strongly condemned Prague for the dismissal of charter signatories from work because of their political views. The International Confederation of Free Trade Unions has also protested official policies in employment and the blatant discrimination against dissidents. The parliamentary assembly of the Council of Europe has declared its solidarity with Charter 77 in recent years. Verbal support has also been forthcoming from various national bodies and some notable Western politicians, including the U.S. Department of State, the French Socialist party, the Norwegian government, the Portuguese Parliament, and a number of British and West German members of parliament. The breadth of international condemnation has had little durable influence on government policy. Prague maintains that it scrupulously observes all important human rights in compliance with international stipulations.

Sympathy for Charter 77 among sections of the Western public has been in evidence, but rarely manifests itself in active support. The Western public has shown interest in the information that the chartists provide and has rebroadcast such texts into Czechoslovakia via Western radio stations, occasionally campaigned against government repression, and provided some material assistance to help keep the civil rights movement buoyant. Several small organizations in the West also supply direct aid to Charter 77, usually channelled through Czechoslovak exiles. It has become almost customary for visiting Western political delegations to plan meetings with charter representatives. In recent years, for example, brief sessions have been arranged with, among others, U.S. Senator Daniel Moynihan, four Austrian People's party parliamentarians, and General Secretary Peter Glotz of the West German Social Democratic Party. Although such meetings often result in repressions after the visitors depart, they help to bolster the domestic and international reputation of Charter 77.

Occasional protest campaigns have been organized in the West to appeal for the release of imprisoned chartists or to oppose major political trials. Western lawyers and other observers arrived in Prague to attend the VONS trial in October 1979, but were refused entry into the courtroom. Despite the Western media's attention to the proceedings, international disapprobation was unable to prevent the passing of long prison terms on the accused. The authorities correctly calculated that the international campaign would eventually expire.

A few protests on behalf of victimized chartists have been successful, but only when the regime has concluded that it was less troublesome to release the person in question than have world attention concentrated on him or her. This was the case with Václav Havel, who, incarcerated in October 1979, became seriously ill and required proper medical treatment. When protests for his release mounted from international PEN clubs, eminent actors, musicians, and playwrights, Havel's sentence was suddenly suspended on medical grounds. Another international protest campaign, involving petitions and substantial media coverage, was staged on behalf of seven human rights activists arrested in May 1981 and scheduled to be tried early in 1982. The protest played some role in securing their premature release and the cancellation of legal proceedings. On this occasion, the authorities were particularly concerned about the negative image they were projecting abroad; a political trial would have damaged their international standing even further. In retrospect, the annulment of the trial did not entail any substantial costs to the regime and did not signify the surrender of any ground to Charter 77. Sporadic international protests have rarely been sustained and usually focus on specific individuals rather than on long-term issues and government policy. The Communist Party authorities are perfectly aware that such interest soon wanes and that the international spotlight often shifts rapidly to another part of the globe.

6

Repression and Reprisal

Verbal Attacks

The attitude of the Prague regime toward Charter 77 has been clearcut from the outset – in official press reports, broadcasts, and speeches. Within days of the charter's appearance, the signatories were vehemently denounced as traitors and agents of Western imperialism. The mass media, the government's mouthpiece, claimed that the chartists consisted of a minute group of discredited reformist politicians and intellectuals lacking any support among the masses, a group that clearly had not refrained from their "ill-fated attempts to sow counterrevolution" in Czechoslovakia. In the almost hysterical propaganda offensive unleashed during the first few weeks of the Charter's appearance, an assortment of communist invectives were employed to categorize the enemy, to justify the methods used in suppressing it, and to isolate Charter 77 from the population by warning the public against supporting it. On January 13, 1977, the Soviet daily *Pravda* reiterated the tone set by *Rudé Právo* the day before, in which Charter 77 was said to have been created "on the orders of anti-communist and Zionist centers by a group drawn from the collapsed Czechoslovak reactionary bourgeoisie and the defeated organizers of the 1968 counterrevolution."

After the initial verbal assault, the Czechoslovak media fell largely silent on the charter, partly to give the impression that the movement had vanished; party leaders rarely hinted about the campaign in their public statements. Nevertheless, to remind the populace that government attitudes have not altered and that the threat of counterrevolution lingers, occasional official analyses of Charter 77 have been made public. A *Rudé Právo* article on October 20, 1979, published in the midst of an intensive anti-charter phase, explained to readers that

> many forces have ganged up in this crusade against Czechoslovakia [including] . . . internal diversionists for whom NATO propaganda jargon has chosen the word "dissidents" . . . people who have not reconciled themselves to their defeat, be it in 1948 or twenty years later. They try to organize anti-state groups, produce inflammatory pamphlets and false rumours, slander society and the state, basically on orders from abroad.

The article warned the public and the West that

> a great error will be made by all those who interpret the process of detente and the Final Act of Helsinki as a blank cheque which commits the socialist countries to release the hands of and widen the scope for counter-revolutionary elements, and to grant them the right to disrupt the socialist state.

To confirm that the chartists would remain subject to persecution and that dialogue with them was out of the question, *Rudé Právo* threatened that the authorities consider it their "sacred duty to protect and guard our achievements . . . . We have enough resoluteness . . . .We have no reason to show weakness or to make concessions."

The regime's position toward the charter has not changed fundamentally during the last decade. Whether it publicly attacks the movement or remains silent depends on various factors. The two chief factors relate to the importance of international public relations and how menacing the regime's judgment on the opposition appears to be at any juncture. There is no reason to suppose that Prague will moderate its stance in the near future or that it will be prepared to reach a *modus vivendi* with its "ideological foes." The CPCS has lucidly defined its attitude toward Charter 77: the campaign is considered an "impertinent interference in the internal affairs of the state . . . an attempt to create a fifth column and upset the situation in Czechoslovakia."[71]

Although the authorities have issued no overt statements about the charter in recent years, state leaders make periodic allusions to the civil rights campaign. During the seventeenth CPCS Congress, held in Prague in March 1986, party leader Gustáv Husák stressed that "socialist legality" must continue to be strengthened and the individual must be protected against "unlawful behavior":

> We will not allow anyone to break our laws and to undermine our political system and socialist order, even if this is done under the guise of the noblest phrases about freedom, democracy, or a so-called fight for human rights.[72]

Chronicle of Repression

The campaign of repression against Charter 77 and related groups has assumed many forms, but has stopped short of the wholesale incarceration of signatories and active supporters. Media campaigns slandering the movement in effect constitute a trial in absentia, in which the accused are denied all means of self-defense. The propaganda offensive has also included character assassinations of leading chartists. The verbal attacks were an important ingredient for mobilizing public opinion against Charter 77. When they failed to produce all the desired results, the authorities calculated that a policy of silence would be more fruitful. Although the majority of the population was effectually discouraged from expressing open support for the restoration of civil liberties, the same people privately could sympathize with the charter once the media had informed them about its existence.

The government has conducted a disinformation campaign against Charter 77, which includes the circulation of fraudulent charter letters and documents. Counterfeit texts produced by the security services are supposed to incriminate the activists, individually or as a group, in terrorist or subversive operations and thus to discredit them in the eyes of the public. A false Charter 77 document was manufactured in 1977 and sent to various addressees to create confusion and mistrust. Equally, it was used to test the reliability of recipients, whose duty as citizens was to report such texts to the police.[73] In December 1981, the security forces disseminated a rumor—repeated by some Western news agencies—that Charter 77 supported martial law as a viable means of solving the crisis in Poland. The report was strenuously denied a few days later in an authentic Charter 77 statement that condemned "any solution to social conflict by military or political force."[74] Several other attempts at disinformation have been tried, including one to discredit the clandestine SRA as kidnappers. The accusation was strongly denied by the SRA in June 1982. The SRA condemned the police provocation and attempts to blackmail the wife of the imprisoned Ladislav Lis. In these attempts she received a threatening letter, purportedly from the SRA, demanding a ransom payment to forestall the abduction of her young daughter.[75]

Unofficial activists have been subject to numerous forms of police harassment: sporadic or round-the-clock surveillance, persistent and often overt bugging of apartments, direct or indirect threats, blackmail attempts, house searches, and the confiscation of private property, such as typewriters, books, and documents. In the past decade, several hundred people have been detained by the police, either for a few hours, days, weeks, or months, and sometimes repeatedly, to discourage them from engaging in "antistate activities." For example, in January 1985, seven charter activists, including several spokespersons, were taken into custody and questioned about certain documents. They refused to answer on the grounds that issuing such texts was not illegal under Czechoslovak law; they were released after 48 hours.

Individuals have been harassed or threatened for an unwillingness to distance themselves from a proscribed person or to collaborate with the police. According to one unofficial document, repressive measures are used against a broad circle of people associated with each Charter 77 signatory, including their closest kin, friends, work colleagues, and neighbors.[76] In a protest letter to Prime Minister Štrougal on May 28, 1985, chartists complained that it had also become standard secret police practice to conduct surveillance of certain citizens during visits by Western statesmen to Czechoslovakia. The conditions of this surveillance "amount to a virtual state of house arrest" in attempts to prevent charter signatories from meeting with members of foreign delegations and the journalists accompanying them. The police also enforce "protective supervision" of well-known "antisocialist activists." These people are required to report to police stations at periodic intervals, and security officers are entitled to enter their homes at any time without a warrant, harass their visitors, and control their private finances and movements. Among the "supervised" individuals are charter signatories Martin Jirous, Jiří Gruntorad, Ladislav Lis, and Jan Litomiský. On the basis of a special law, "protective surveillance" of recently released political inmates is becoming more commonplace.[77]

During police detention, activists are routinely interrogated – sometimes for long hours – and often insulted, degraded, and threatened. Nearly all the original charter signatories have undergone interrogation at some stage, and a few have reported being physically mistreated while in custody during the course of intensive questioning. Karel Soukop, a member of the collective of Charter 77 spokespersons, was beaten both prior to his interrogation in September 1981 and following questioning in his apartment when he refused to discuss his contacts and activities. Similarly, Zdena Tominová, former spokeswoman, was assaulted by police officers and apparently threatened with rape in October 1981.[78] Physical attacks on chartists have also been carried out by "unknown persons"; the culprits are never apprehended but indications have shown that security forces masterminded the incidents.

Although Czechoslovakia ratified the International Covenant on Civil and Political Rights, which stipulates the standards governing pretrial detention that are also contained in domestic civil rights legislation, the guarantees are frequently violated. Confidential instructions issued by party and security organs are commonly applied against political dissenters and override any strictly legal requirements. Instructions can include unwarranted detentions, long detentions without trial, the returning of individuals to custody pending further trial, and the retention of charges against people released from custody – where a legal limbo is deliberately imposed. Arbitrary arrests often occur prior to some important national anniversary or before the visit of a foreign dignitary. This happened during Leonid Brezhnev's visit to Prague in May 1978 on the excuse that demonstrations or terrorist acts could have been planned by the detainees. Similar pretexts have been used to place individuals under house arrest for varying spells and provide an effective tool in preventing contacts with Western politicians and journalists.

Human rights activists have faced both political and criminal trials. "Political justice" has been used selectively by the authorities, because it is usually highly visible and can have adverse international repercussions. Some analysts of Soviet bloc repression contend that the government carefully weighs the costs and benefits before staging a political trial.[79] The benefits include the neutralization of an opponent, the poignant warning thereby sent to his or her supporters, and the public confirmation that certain behavior is classified as subversive and will not be tolerated. The costs involve an acknowledgement of the existence of opposition, valuable publicity for the regime's opponents, and the creation of an additional pretext for protests. As a result, the Czechoslovak regime has only opted for "political justice" against certain prominent dissidents. There appears to be some deliberation at high political levels before a defendent is brought to trial. This may have been the case with four leading chartists who were held in custody for five months before their trial and conviction in October 1979. Since the early 1980s, however, blatantly political trials have become more rare, because the authorities are conscious of the damage such trials inflict on their international prestige.

Political trials have occasionally been disguised as criminal processes, in which the accused are denied any claims to political prisoner status. These trials commonly involve lesser-known activists, because criminal proceedings against prominent charter personalities would be viewed with profound suspicion. Criminal prosecution would include both fabricated charges (including offenses such as theft, perjury, or embezzlement) and the interpretation of political acts as criminal offenses. Jiří Gruntorad, Jan Wunsch, and Ivan Jirous were tried and sentenced in this way. Conducting criminal trials seems to be less costly for the regime, and it has therefore reverted to them more frequently in the last decade. The use of criminal trials contributes to the regime's portrayal of civil rights activism as criminal or deviant behavior.

Dozens of people have received prison sentences for monitoring human rights abuses and distributing unofficial documents; the sentences have ranged from a few months to several years. According to a VONS communiqué released in December 1983, 21 people were serving sentences for independent activities while 47 more people received suspended convictions or were being systematically persecuted outside of prison. In addition, VONS reported on 149 individuals who had served their sentences or whose offenses were no longer being investigated. In some cases, incarcerated political offenders have received additional convictions for "new crimes" committed while inside. VONS representatives admitted that they can obtain the necessary documentation on only "a fraction of cases of court repression, or of repressions which did not end up in the courtroom."[80] A U.S. presidential report issued in late 1983 confirmed that "the number of persons held in detention is probably fewer than one hundred, but can fluctuate substantially."[81] At that time the number of political inmates serving sentences probably numbered between 30 and 50. VONS estimated in 1985 that the authorities were still holding 17 political prisoners after a prolonged period during which such visible persecution of chartists was eased.

In May 1985, on the fortieth anniversary of the end of World War II, the Czechoslovak president decreed a limited amnesty that embraced a number of political prisoners. At least four prominent dissidents were freed before completing their sentences, but the amnesty specifically excluded inmates convicted of seeking to leave the country without official permission and did not revoke the "protective surveillance" orders imposed on several known oppositionists. VONS also pointed out that amnesty was not given to people serving sentences in the second and third penal categories "for their beliefs or for acts which followed from their convictions, or were sentenced as a result of criminal proceedings which arouse legal, political or moral doubts." The dissident community generally was disappointed by the scope of the 1985 amnesty. Accurate statistics on the political prisoner population are practically impossible to obtain, particularly because the government does not recognize prisoners of conscience and does not issue figures on political inmates. Furthermore, by releasing individuals on parole with a suspended sentence, the authorities are able to keep them under observation, maintain the constant threat of imprisonment, and avoid too much unfavorable publicity.

Prison conditions have also been a serious cause for distress. In 1982, Amnesty International voiced concern about reports from two jails where politicals were incarcerated. In Mirov prison the inmates labored in a workshop without adequate protective aid against asbestos dust, while in Minkovice prison they received an inadequate diet and lived in unhygienic conditions.[82] In 1983 there were reports that the treatment of prisoners of conscience had deteriorated. There were several reported cases of prison guards beating political inmates or purposely disregarding their health by denying them medical attention.[83] Some chartists, including Jiří Gruntorad and Jiří Wolf, have been held in third category prisons, which are usually reserved for the most dangerous criminals. In June 1982, Charter 77 appealed to the Czechoslovak Federal Assembly for a full investigation into prison conditions.[84] The chartists asked for a special commission to assess working conditions in jails, real working hours, wages, the treatment of inmates by guards, the implementation of the right to education, and freedom of religious practice in prisons. They requested remedies to the abuses experienced by both political and nonpolitical prisoners. The authorities did not respond to the appeal.

The regime uses several administrative measures against dissidents to make their lives unpleasant or unbearable. In the highly bureaucratized communist system such forms of harassment add to the already frustrating everyday problems experienced by the average citizen. Administrative repression includes job demotion or dismissal, because officials may deprive a person of employment if they publicly express disagreement with state policies. A dissident may also have his or her telephone disconnected, postal communications discontinued, a driving license withdrawn, a car confiscated. A dissident can be expelled from a labor union or other public organization, excluded from participation in official artistic, cultural, or scientific activities, and denied health care and other welfare benefits. A dissident's children may be deprived of educational opportunities. Security service persecution is supplemented with discrimination by employers and government departments.

One of the main forms of discrimination against people holding dissident opinions is to ban them from all important positions in the civil service, in economic institutions, and in the cultural and scientific fields. Moreover, in some cases individuals have been evicted from their homes, separated from their families, and forced to find accommodations far from their native cities, families, and friends. The authorities may also seize passports and deny individuals the special permits required to travel abroad or the exit permits needed to emigrate. The dissidents' families often suffer similar reprisals.

Cases of psychiatric repression in Czechoslovakia have also emerged. Although the practice is evidently not as widespread as in the Soviet Union, there have been incidents when medically sane individuals have been "treated" in psychiatric institutions. The Catholic activist Augustin Navrátil was confined to a psychiatric hospital after attempting to collect signatures for a petition protesting against breaches of religious rights.[85] In January 1986, Navrátil was reported to have been held in a psychiatric clinic since December 1985 following his arrest on charges of "incitement against the state." At least one other unofficial peace movement activist has been subjected to similar persecution In January 1985, a Blansko District Court enforced "protective psychiatric treatment" on Jan Pukalík, who in November 1983 had collected signatures among citizens in the Blansko area protesting against the siting of nuclear missiles in Czechoslovakia.[86]

A few charter signatories have been forcibly expatriated, usually following substantial pressure in which their lives or health were threatened. Zdena Freundová, a VONS activist and former member of the Charter 77 collective, was sexually molested, beaten, interrogated, threatened by police, and forced to emigrate in June 1982. Forced emigration is usually applied against dissidents whom the regime apparently considers too dangerous a source of opposition to allow to remain in the country. Between 100 and 150 Charter signatories have left the country since 1977;

the majority were pressured to emigrate by the police. After emigration or expulsion, their citizenship is usually taken away and they are barred from returning. In many cases these exiles have helped to publicize the activities of Charter 77 in their host countries.

The authorities have also perpetrated or approved of direct physical assault, which, in at least two recorded incidents, have resulted in the victim's death. In February 1981, the mutilated body of Přemysl Coufal, a secretly ordained Catholic priest thought to be a senior member of the unofficial church, was discovered in his apartment in Bratislava. Police involvement was strongly suspected, though the authorities claimed he had committed suicide. During the weeks preceding his death, Coufal had been interrogated several times, but refused to sign a pledge of cooperation with the police.[87] Pavel Švanda, a practicing Catholic, was found dead near Brno in October 1981. The results of his autopsy were never revealed, though officials asserted that he had jumped into a cave to his death. During Father Václav Malý's interrogation in January 1982 (he was a Charter 77 spokesman at that time), the police threatened to have him killed in a rigged car accident and pointedly reminded him of what had happened to Švanda.[88]

Government Maneuvers

Prague's overall objective with regard to Charter 77 and other unofficial groupings, both before and since 1977, has remained constant – to stifle, subdue, and eliminate. The flexible elements in government policy are the timetable and the methods used at any particular juncture. In early 1977, the regime believed that Charter 77 could be eliminated swiftly through a combination of media vilification and the arrest of the most prominent organizers. When this failed and the movement survived, the government opted for a more prolonged war of attrition – hoping to harass and exhaust the chartists into oblivion. Simultaneously, they endeavored to isolate the campaign by undercutting the charter's contacts with the population. Officials calculated that if the movement could be confined to a segment of the intellectual community, the immediate threat would be minimized and eventually dwindle away. Although the government has partially succeeded in this policy, the possibility remains that if social and economic conditions were to deteriorate substantially various independent movements could obtain a wider popular resonance.

Intense repressive campaigns are usually mounted when the regime is less concerned about international public opinion or feels either emboldened or threatened domestically. The anti-Charter 77 drive was intensive throughout 1981, when officials were apprehensive that the effects of the Polish conflict might spill across the border. Once the perceived danger subsided, the campaign largely died down, though it has never been fully discontinued. There is little doubt that the government has not seriously contemplated accepting the chartists' offer of a dialogue. Such compromises, involving the prospect of genuine political reforms, would endanger the *status quo* on which their power ultimately rests.

In its war of attrition, Prague has used several tactics with varying degrees of success. Officials have attempted to decimate the front ranks of the human rights movement through arrests, harassment, and forced exile. Although a number of chartists were thereby eliminated from the scene, the movement was rarely short of replacements. Attempts to destroy Charter 77 from within, by exploiting differences between various individuals and groups, also failed. For example, the officially cultivated rumor that Petr Uhl and the "revolutionary socialists" possessed munition dumps and planned acts of terrorism was widely disbelieved. Undoubtedly, the security service also planted informers within the movement. They could report on the Charter's work, but they were never effective as *agents provocateurs*.

The authorities have proved more adept at intimidating some of the lesser-known signatories and supporters through police actions, imprisonment, or administrative measures. But the campaign was not comprehensive enough to embrace all the signatories simultaneously. Such an operation would have proved too politically costly and visible and most likely provoke international condemnation. It would also provide Charter 77 with substantial publicity without any guarantee of successfully quelling the movement. Officials evidently decided that behind-the-scenes methods would prove more productive in the long term. Concurrently, they would launch attacks on VONS and other charter-related initiatives to lop off the various branches of the human rights campaign. Such a policy fell short of expectations, because Prague seemingly underestimated the number of people willing to persist with unofficial work on behalf of civil liberties.

Although the regime has contributed to assuring the limited size of Charter 77, it has also been faced with a religious revival and a passive rebellion among the young, partly inspired by the activities of the chartists. It has therefore tried to minimize the potential for religion and culture evolving into focal points for opposition. The persecution of priests, lay Christian activists, and young nonconformist rock musicians testifies to this policy. Such repression may need to be intensified in the future, although its results could backfire by stimulating further protests and even more outright forms of dissent.

To restrict the charter's accomplishments, Prague has endeavored to sever chartists' links with the West while projecting the impression that the human rights campaign has been discontinued. For the most part this ploy has been deficient, even though contacts between chartists and their Western supporters have been persistently hindered. In light of 10 years of evidence, temporary improvements in the government's treatment of the opposition should be viewed as tactical measures partially intended to disarm Western criticism. Improvements are usually evident prior to or during visits by diplomatic or important trade delegations, or during an official Czechoslovak visit abroad. As witnessed during Husák's visit to Vienna in November 1982, public trials are avoided on such occasions and open harassment decreases. Strong criticism of Prague's human rights record by Western politicians, following their trips to Czechoslovakia, occasionally induce the regime to employ more subtle means to silence dissent. In such instances officials will tend to rely on brief detentions and house searches rather than on imprisonment and physical abuse.

The Czech government also seems to take into account concurrent Soviet policy regarding its own opposition. A major crackdown in the USSR often has been followed by similar campaigns in the satellite countries. Furthermore, specific methods applied against dissidents by the Soviet security service are imitated by its Czechoslovak counterpart. For example, judicial repression through closed criminal trials gained prominence throughout the Soviet bloc in the 1970s after its initial application in the USSR. Domestic repressive campaigns often appear to be coordinated between Communist states; even certain tactics may be worked out at high security levels. With the imposition of martial law in Poland in December 1981, Czechoslovakia simultaneously directed a nationwide mobilization of militia and secret service forces against the dissident community.

Since 1982, particularly after the situation in Poland had been "stabilized" and "normalized" and with Prague hoping to bolster its image in the West, direct forms of persecution have been eased somewhat. There have been fewer reports of police beatings or suspicious deaths, but other forms of repression against political and religious dissidents continue to operate. The regime seems to have developed a strategy of differentiation between the various elements of the dissident scene and applied more pressure on those individuals or groups that are perceived as posing a greater immediate threat to its interests. This may help explain why recent persecution has focused more on religious activists than on political dissidents and human rights campaigners. Such policies, however, are always subject to change depending on the regime's current political requirements.

Although the precise tactics the regime will use in the future are difficult to predict, the long-term objective certainly is the elimination of Charter 77 and other autonomous movements, and the extension, preservation, and consolidation of Communist Party hegemony in all spheres of public life.

7

Conclusions and Prospects

Two important observations can be made on the basis of the experience of Charter 77 during its 10-year history. First, on the basis of the Prague government's record, the likelihood of wide-ranging internal political and economic reform in Czechoslovakia remains slight. The entrenched Communist party leadership is unlikely to change its policies fundamentally, and the chances for serious dialogue and compromise with the human rights campaigners are as remote as they were in 1977. Top leadership changes, following the replacement of the aging Gustáv Husák are unlikely to affect this prognosis in any significant way. The regime is generally uncompromising in dealing with critics, though for certain tactical reasons, especially on the international arena, its repression has sometimes assumed milder forms.

A second significant observation is that a mass protest movement has not materialized during the past decade and is unlikely to emerge in the foreseeable future. Although Charter 77 enjoys widespread sympathy among the population, the number of active supporters — whether signatories or not — has remained relatively small — probably totaling no more than a few thousand individuals. Involvement in any "alternative structures" of "citizens' initiatives," as proposed by the chartists, has also been restricted. The majority of Czechoslovak society tends to be passive in its relations with the regime. Seeing little immediate prospect for improvement, people have withdrawn into their private lives rather than risk involvement in dissident activities. Citizens are familiar with the government's repressive policies against opponents and critics and choose to air their grievances in private for fear of endangering their own and their children's future. Nevertheless, a sizable and expanding "underground church" and an apparently thriving youth-oriented "underground culture" testify to the breadth and persistence of more hidden forms of potential opposition to the Prague government.

The short-term prospects, at least until the end of the 1980s, for far-reaching socioeconomic and political reforms and similarly for large-scale political opposition appear to be slight. The orthodox party and government leadership, installed after the 1968 Warsaw Pact invasion, will continue to hold power and will eventually be replaced by younger cadres who may or may not be more inclined to press for some kind of limited reform, which would not, however, undermine their political prerogatives. The apparatus of coercion and the pervasive system of social controls, upon which Communist Party rule ultimately depends, will clearly not be dismantled and may even be extended to prevent or subdue protests emanating from growing popular grievances. The seventeenth CPCS Congress in March 1986 confirmed such an appraisal. No major leadership changes or significant policy alterations were announced, and no liberalization in the realm of human rights and civil liberties was in the offing.

A thorough, market-oriented economic reform, for which some chartists have been striving, involving substantial industrial modernization and the decentralization of decision making, seems unlikely. The limited concessions recently allowed to certain sectors of the economy, including agriculture and the service industry, and other minor adjustments to the system, clearly do not venture far enough to offer substantially improved prospects.[89] It is probably too early to judge the impact of Mikhail Gorba chev's accession in Moscow on any Czechoslovak reforms. But party leaders continue to stress that market solutions will be rejected; the "leading role of the Communist Party" will not be jeopardized. Instead, any economic reforms are to consist of "modernizing" the system of planning, whereby greater decision making will be delegated to individual enterprises, but the important strategic decisions will continue to be made at the center.[90] Some Western analysts have described such alterations as a form of "streamlining" the orthodox, centrally-planned system, but not imitating the more flexible Hungarian model.

The long-term prospects are more problematic to forecast, because numerous interrelated variables must be considered – including developments in the Soviet Union, East–West relations, and the ability of the Soviet bloc economies to weather their growing crises. Nevertheless, it is fairly safe to assume that without sweeping changes in the USSR there are only limited possibilities for political, social, or economic progress in Czechoslovakia. Human rights, as understood in international conventions, are unlikely to be respected to any greater extent than they have been since 1968, even though Prague may not consider it expedient to initiate whole-scale purges and mass terror on the scale of the Stalinist 1950s or in the aftermath of the Prague Spring. Any temporary improvements in civil liberties can always be canceled when it suits the leadership. The authorities may even be willing to tolerate the existence of a "dissident community," as long as the movement for independent social action does not appear to take root among the working masses or challenge the party's political programs. In the absence of democratic checks and balances on important decision making and actions, the government will continue to act arbitrarily to protect its interests. To introduce practically any of the charter's reformist propositions into official policy could significantly improve civil rights and living conditions, but the authorities evidently fear that this would constitute a first step toward dismantling the one-party system.

It is highly probable that Charter 77 and its various

spin-offs will persist regardless of the persecution. Concurrently, any meaningful advancement of human rights appears unlikely. The last decade has amply demonstrated that in a totalitarian political system, peaceable, law-abiding protest benefiting from an international mandate can assure the best chances for the long-term survival of a dissident movement, particularly in the absence of overt mass support. The chartists will persevere in the hope of stimulating more widespread public involvement in autonomous social activities. But without far-reaching international and domestic transformations, Charter 77 alone probably cannot spark a mass movement for democratization on the scale of the Prague Spring or of Poland's Solidarity. On the other hand, a gradually deteriorating economy, stagnating or deteriorating living standards, and increasing social frustrations could eventually engender the growth of autonomous public initiatives and even more substantive forms of political opposition in Czechoslovakia.

Postscript

Five members of the outlawed Jazz Section of the Musicians Union were tried in Prague at the beginning of March 1987. In the light of adverse international publicity surrounding the trial, and in the shadow of Gorbachev's *glasnost* campaign, the Czechoslovak prosecutor handed out more lenient convictions than observers had expected. Jazz Section chairman Karel Srp received a 16-month jail term (minus the six months he has already spent in prison), his deputy Vladimír Kouřil 10 months (minus 6 already served), while the remaining defendants—Česmir Hunst, Tomaš Křivanek, and Jozef Skalnik—were given suspended sentences and placed on probation for up to four years.

Current developments in the Soviet Union are evidently creating ripples in several East European states. In Czechoslovakia they could nudge a more reform-minded element within the Communist Party leadership to press for further "restructuring" of the domestic economy. This could also embolden Charter 77 to seek greater public support for more far-reaching liberalization and democratization of the ossified system of government. In a "Letter to Signatories," dated January 6, 1987 and signed by eight Charter 77 activists (including the three current spokespersons—Libusé Šilhanova, Josef Vohřysek, and Jan Litomišsky), a proposal was put forward for "a new, wider, and probably more political program that corresponds better to the present state of affairs in the country."

March 1987

Notes

1. Charter 77, "Statement on the 17th Anniversary of August 21, 1968" (Prague, August 20, 1985).

2. For a valuable summary and analysis of post-Prague Spring Czechoslovakia see Sonia A. Winter, "The Sovietization of Czechoslovakia, 1968–1983," *Radio Free Europe Research* (RFER), Background Report no. 196 (Munich, August 16, 1983).

3. For further details on "normalization," Czechoslovak style, see Vladimír V. Kusin, *From Dubček to Charter 77* (Edinburgh: Q Press, 1978) and Otto Ulc, "The Normalization of Post-Invasion Czechoslovakia," *Survey* 24 (Summer 1979):201–213.

4. Zdeněk Mlynář, "Normalization in Czechoslovakia after 1968," *Crises in Soviet-Type Systems*, Study no. 1 (Köln: Index, 1982).

5. Charter 77, *Document No.9/85: On the Fortieth Anniversary of the End of World War Two.*

6. For details on the opposition movement during this period refer to Kusin *From Dubček to Charter 77*, 145–169.

7. Quoted in H. Gordon Skilling, *Charter 77 and Human Rights in Czechoslovakia* (London: Allen & Unwin, 1981), 13.

8. Charter 77, *Declaration*, January 1, 1977.

9. The term "chartists" will be used throughout this account for those individuals who signed Charter 77 or have actively supported the movement.

10. Ibid.

11. Ibid.

12. For summaries of Charter 77 documents on these and other human rights violations see the appendix.

13. Charter 77, *Communiqué*, September 21, 1977.

14. Charter 77, *Informace O Chartě 77*, March 1984.

15. Quoted in Charter 77, *Document No.2/85*, January 7, 1985.

16. Much of the biographical data in this section was supplied by Radio Free Europe in Munich and the Palach Press in London. Some of the facts are difficult to confirm, and the information on some spokespersons is scant and incomplete.

17. The occupational, gender, and residential profile of the signatories is based largely on statistics taken from Radio Free Europe, the Palach Press, a number of Charter 77 documents, and Skilling, *Charter 77 and Human Rights in Czechoslovakia.*

18. Some of the information in this section was supplied by the Palach Press Limited in London, in an unpublished paper by Jan Kavan, which was completed in 1983.

19. Skilling, *Charter 77 and Human Rights in Czechoslovakia*, 127.

20. RFER, *Czechoslovak Situation Report* no. 1 (Munich, January 22, 1982).

21. Jan Patočka, "What Can We Expect From Charter 77?" (Prague, March 8, 1977).

22. U.S. Helsinki Watch Committee, "The Crackdown in Czechoslovakia: Background Information," *Helsinki Watch Committee Report* (New York: U.S. Helsinki Watch Committee, January 1982).

23. "Information Telephoned from Prague: Five Years of Charter 77" (Prague, January 1982).

24. *Palach Press Bulletin No.21/22/23* (London, February 1983).

25. These contributors are often experts in their field. For example, appended to Charter 77, *Document No.6/84*, of March 12, 1984, was a 15-page paper entitled "Dynamics or Stagnation: Notes on the State of the Economy in 1983, and the Plan for 1984," written by Professor Vladimír Kadlec, former rector of the Prague School of Economics and minister of education in the Alexander Dubček government in 1968.

26. Charter 77, *Document No.19/85: Ten Years After Helsinki.*

27. Most texts relating to the work of Charter 77 have been reproduced in the Czech emigré publications *Listy* (Rome), *Studie*

(Rome), and *Svědectví* (Paris). Selected materials are also included in Vilém Prečan, ed., *Kniha Charty* (Köln: Index, 1977), and *Křest'ané a Charta 77* (Köln: Index, 1980).

28. Recent Czechoslovak *samizdat* publications have included the periodicals *Texty*, *Prostor*, the literary quarterly *Kritický Sborník*, *KIFU* (the magazine of the Society for the Distribution of Information in Czechoslovakia), *OBSAH* (collections of literary essays), *Vokno* ("A magazine for the second and other culture"), *Jednou Nohou* ("An independent cultural revue"), *Komentáře*, *Střední Evropa*, *Diskuse*, *Paraf*, and *Solidarnosc* (focusing on events in Poland).

29. For a full account of political discrimination in the educational system see Vratislav Pechota, "Science and Humanities in Czechoslovakia," an unpublished paper (May 1983).

30. Charter 77, *Document No.24/85*, September 25, 1985. One of the signatories to this document was the 1984 Nobel prize winner for literature, Jaroslav Seifert.

31. For more discussion see Skilling, *Charter 77 and Human Rights in Czechoslovakia*, 113–114.

32. Quoted in Charter 77, *Informace o Chartě 77*, March 1984.

33. Charter 77, *Document No.9/85*. For a helpful summary and assessment of this document see RFER, *Czechoslovak Situation Report* no. 9 (Munich, June 3, 1985).

34. Ibid.

35. For a recent list of VONS members see VONS, *Statement No.400: Summary of Cases Monitored by VONS*, November 8, 1984.

36. Preparatory Committee of Free Labor Unions in Czechoslovakia, letter to the 10th All-Trade Union Congress, cited by Palach Press Limited (London), April 14, 1982.

37. Ibid.

38. Preparatory Committee of Free Labor Unions in Czechoslovakia, statement cited by Palach Press Limited (London), November 14, 1982.

39. Ibid.

40. Revolutionary Action Group, statement cited by Palach Press Limited (London), December 15, 1981.

41. Revolutionary Action Group, statement cited by Palach Press Limited (London), April 24, 1982. This statement was signed "CID Press," Campaign Against Dictatorship.

42. For a comprehensive review of "alternative rock music" in

Czechoslovakia and the government's efforts to suppress it, see Charter 77, *Document No.31/83*, August 31, 1983.

43. A full account of this incident is related in VONS, *Statement No.341b: Police and Judicial Repression in Place of Rock Music*, October 11, 1983.

44. The conflict between the Jazz Section of the Union of Czech Musicians and the administration is described in the "Circular Sent by the Young Music Section of the Musicians Union to its Supporters" (Prague, July 20, 1984), cited by Palach Press (London).

45. For more recent details of travails of the Jazz Section see RFER, *Czechoslovak Situation Report* no. 15 (Munich, November 14, 1986).

46. For an up-to-date analysis of this phenomenon refer to RFER, *Czechoslovak Situation Report* no. 5 (Munich, March 26, 1986).

47. *Rudé Právo*, March 28, 1986.

48. Charter 77, *Informace O Chartě 77*, August 1985.

49. Charter 77, *Document No.31/83: On Popular Music*, August 30, 1983.

50. Ibid.

51. For a valuable summary of the persecution of religious orders in Czechoslovakia see Charter 77, *Document No.31/84*, December 12, 1984. A useful account of the government's recent antireligious measures is also contained in the U.S. Department of State, *19th Semiannual Report on the Implementation of the Helsinki Final Act*, April 1, 1985–October 1, 1985, pp. 13–14.

52. Among the outlawed religious sects are the Jehovah's Witnesses. Several members have been incarcerated for various periods because of "illegal religious activity."

53. See Antonín Kratochvil, "The Church in Czechoslovakia," RFER, Background Report no. 78 (Munich, March 30, 1982). VONS regularly chronicles official persecution of religious believers in various parts of the country and makes this information available in its documents.

54. An irregular Slovak religious periodical, *Náboženstvo a Sučastnost* (Religion and the Present), has also appeared since 1985. At least four issues have been published by an unknown dissident group, purportedly based in Bratislava.

55. For an account of this police operation see RFER, *Czechoslovak Situation Report* no. 11 (Munich, June 24, 1983).

56. *Amnesty International Report 1985* (London: Amnesty International Publications, 1985), 281–282.

57. The Velehrad celebrations are described in RFER, *Czechoslovak Situation Report* no. 12 (Munich, July 15, 1985). Among the positive repercussions of the event was the publication in March 1986 of a new *samizdat* periodical entitled *Velehrad* that features articles by theologians and philosophers.

58. For some details on the campaign see RFER, *Czechoslovak Situation Report* no. 9 (Munich, June 18, 1986).

59. As reported by *Studie* (Rome), no. 71 (1980), 482–485.

60. *Charter 77 On Peace* (London: Palach Press Limited, 1983). Palach Press Limited also published a booklet entitled *Voices From Prague*, edited by Jan Kavan and Zdena Tomin, that contains documents on Czechoslovakia and the peace movement.

61. Charter 77, *Document No.27/82.*

62. RFER, *Czechoslovak Situation Report* no. 20 (Munich, December 12, 1983).

63. For some details on the incident see RFER, *Czechoslovak Situation Report* no. 5 (Munich, March 26, 1986).

64. Charter 77, *Document No.5/85*, March 11, 1985. This document was signed by 45 people, including all the current spokespersons and many former ones. Since it was released, 21 more individuals have appended their signatures.

65. See Charter 77, *Document No.13/84: Open Letter to the Third Convention on European Nuclear Disarmament* (the convention was held in Perugia, Italy in July 1984).

66. Charter 77, *Document No.9/84*, May 1, 1984.

67. Charter 77, *Document No.19/84*, November 2, 1984.

68. According to the Polish underground newsletter *Tygodnik Mazowsze*, no. 175 (Warsaw, July 2, 1986), 1.

69. The communiqué was dated October 23, 1986 and released simultaneously in Budapest, Berlin (GDR), Prague, and Warsaw.

70. Charter 77, *Document No.39/83*, November 14, 1983.

71. See the Czechoslovak Communist Party's Central Committee theoretical and political monthly *Nova Mysl*, no. 5 (May 1980), 18–38.

72. For a summary of the 17th CPCS Congress see RFER, *Czechoslovak Situation Report* no. 6 (Munich, April 16, 1986).

73. *The American Bulletin*, no. 306 (Cicero, Ill.: Czechoslovak National Council of America, August 1982).

74. Charter 77, *Charter 77 Statement*, January 7, 1982.

75. Revolutionary Action Group, *Coordinating Committee of the Revolutionary Action Group Statement*, cited by Palach Press Limited (London, June 8, 1982).

76. See Charter 77, *Informace o Chartĕ 77*, March 1984.

77. For an assessment of "protective surveillance" as it applies to Czechoslovak citizens see Charter 77, *Document No.8/84*, April 6, 1984.

78. *Amnesty International Report 1982* (London: Amnesty International Publications, 1982), 261.

79. See Robert Sharlet, "Dissent and Repression in the Soviet Union and Eastern Europe: Changing Patterns Since Khruschev," *International Journal* 33, no. 4 (Autumn 1978).

80. VONS, *Communiqué No. 349*, December 6, 1983.

81. Fifteenth Semiannual Report by the President to the Commission on Security and Cooperation in Europe, on the Implementation of the Helsinki Final Act, June 1–November 30, 1983.

82. *Amnesty International Report 1982* (London: Amnesty International Publications, 1982), 261.

83. Vladimír V. Kusin, "Czechoslovakia in 1983," RFER, Background Report no. 1 (Munich, January 12, 1984) and *Amnesty International Report 1984* (London: Amnesty International Publications, 1984), 278.

84. Charter 77, *Document No.22/82: Letter to the Federal Assembly of Czechoslovakia* requesting an investigation into the situation in prisons, June 21, 1982.

85. See Skilling, *Charter 77 and Human Rights in Czechoslovakia*, 137.

86. VONS, *Statement No.423: Concerning the Jan Pukalík case*, February 21, 1985.

87. For details see the West German daily, *Die Welt*, on March 24, 1983, summarized in RFER, *Czechoslovak Situation Report* no. 20 (Munich, November 23, 1984).

88. For details consult a compilation of materials by Vilém Prečan, *Human Rights in Czechoslovakia: A Documentation, September 1981–December 1982* (Paris: International Committee for the Support of Charter 77 in Czechoslovakia, April 1983).

89. For an analysis of the economic situation drafted by "a group of experts" on behalf of Charter 77, see Charter 77, *Document No.28/85*, November 14, 1985. The document suggests that

a group of experienced economists should be permitted to formulate specific proposals for improving the structure and performance of the national economy.

90. Several recent documents analyzing the country's economic woes have been written by Vladimír Kadlec, a prominent economist, and published in *samizdat* under the auspices of Charter 77. In particular, see Charter 77, *Document No.6/84*, available from Palach Press Limited (London) and two documents entitled "We Live in Debt, Have Mortgaged Our Future, and are Eating up our Reserves" (September 1984) and "The Economy in 1988" (1984).

Appendix

Summary of Selected Charter 77 Documents

The following is a selection of 23 Charter 77 documents, focusing on some of the most important problems currently facing Czechoslovakia as seen through the eyes of the opposition movement. The documents have been summarized and placed in the chronological order in which they were first released.

Document No. 7/ 1977: Social and Economic Rights

There is widespread hidden unemployment in Czechoslovakia, together with an obligation to work and a curtailment of the right to resign or change jobs. Labor legislation and labor policy are deteriorating. There is a high level of female employment because of economic pressures when the husband's income cannot ensure a decent standard of living. Women are discriminated against in the assignment of posts and wages. The "personal work appraisal" places political involvement above professional skills or work output. The "cadre nomenclature" gives preferential treatment to party members and unjustly discriminates against non-members. Labor unions do not function freely, are run by the CPCS apparatus, and do not protect workers' interests. Working hours rank among the [longest] in Europe. When workers are denied civil and political rights, negative repercussions appear throughout economic and social life.

Document No. 22/ 1977: Development of Nuclear Energy in Czechoslovakia

Environmental hazards and low safety standards prevail in the nuclear energy program; official standards, which fall below those enforced in the West, are not being observed in practice. The main reason for this condition is Czechoslovakia's dependence on the Soviet Union for equipment that is unsuited to the country's high population density. Official secrecy surrounding nuclear energy projects prevents proper evaluation by experts. Two major accidents led to deaths and contamination of a stream; poor working conditions and long shifts contributed to the accidents. Future deployment of nuclear energy should be opened to public debate.

Document No. 24/ 1977: Freedom to Travel Abroad

Freedom of travel is an important right guaranteed by the constitution and by the International Covenant on Civil and Political Rights. But Czechoslovak legislation negates this right, when a citizen who wishes to travel abroad is dependent on the judgment of a state agency or employer. A travel document may be withheld if the journey is not in accord with state interests. The minister of the interior has complete freedom to interpret principles laid down by the law. Legal action is taken against citizens who stay abroad without official permission; conviction can include imprisonment and confiscation of property. Sanctions may be applied against relatives of people who have emigrated.

Document No. 26/ 1977: Consumer Problems

The inadequate quantity and poor quality of goods and services and the consumption-oriented life-style of the masses are linked to the lack of political democracy and the absence of popular control over economic decision making. The "second economy" (bribery, barter, black market, etc.) exerts a demoralizing influence. Only the privileged elite, possessing high incomes and access to special shops, is spared these difficulties. Education and health-care service are grossly underdeveloped. A consumers' organization should be formed to defend their interests, and full information on the economy must be made available to the public.

Document—May 5, 1980: The Problems of Pensioners

Society's attitude toward persons who cannot work is an important indicator of its humaneness. Old-age pensions should be increased and guaranteed to keep pace with the cost of living. On average, pensioners take a 43 percent cut in income after retirement; most of the pension is spent on food. Wide social differences exist between rich and poor, and an increasing proportion of the poor are pensioners.

Document No. 6/ 1982: Price Increases and the Economic Situation

The 1982 price increases on basic foods severely interfered with the population's standard of living and was an admission of the unsatisfactory state of the economy. Living standards of families with children are 40 percent lower than those of childless families. Ten percent of all households earn less than the subsistence level, and 10 percent share a dwelling unit with other families. Citizens should be told about the causes of unachieved economic plans, material losses, and serious shortages of goods. A radical change in the structure of the economy is imperative.

Document No. 7/ 1982: Discrimination
Against Writers

A large proportion of literature cannot be published, and many authors have no possibility of publishing their work because of an undeclared ban. Their means of subsistence are often too limited to permit a decent standard of living. More authors are in prison now than five years ago. A list of 230 silenced authors is attached to the document.

Documents No. 8 and 11/ 1982: Freedom
of Conviction and Religious Rights

Charter 77 calls for the respect for various rights relating to religious practice: assembly in churches and religious societies, communicating and publishing religious views, rights of parents to allow children to acquire religious convictions, abolition of state supervision over religious instruction, freedom to study theology without interference, respect for autonomy of churches and their contacts abroad, equality of churches and religious societies with other organizations, and equality of church members with other citizens at work and in public life. The current trend favors a further intensification of the antireligious campaign. The year 1981 was a major one for antireligious trials and the criminalization of innocent religious activities.

Document No. 13/ 1982: Attitude toward
Peace Movements

Charter 77 has a positive attitude toward the peace efforts of ordinary citizens. But to safeguard peace it is imperative to end violence and injustice within states. It is difficult to believe in the genuineness of peace efforts when fundamental human and civil rights are suppressed or when such suppression is tacitly accepted or approved. The unofficial citizens' initiatives have more competence to develop peace initiatives than the official bodies.

Document No. 14/ 1982: On the Czechoslovak Legal Code

In March 1976 the government ratified the International Covenant on Civil and Political Rights, and it became a part of Czechoslovak law. Nevertheless, many parts of the legal code contradict these international provisions. The practices of the police, the judiciary, and other bodies violate these provisions. For example, in proceedings against Charter 77 signatories, the judiciary claims that Articles 112 ("damaging Czechoslovak interests abroad") and 98 ("subversion of the Republic") of the penal code override article 19 of the international covenant that guarantees the right of political opposition. The chartists propose specific steps that the Supreme Court should take to amend those sections that are in violation of international provisions and to ensure that the police, judiciary, and other bodies act in accordance with the letter of the law.

Document No. 17/ 1982: Discrimination at Work

In 1969–1970 hundreds of thousands of citizens lost their jobs on political or religious grounds. A second wave of persecution began in 1977 against Charter 77 signatories. The government has not acquainted people with International Labor Organization (ILO) criticisms of working conditions in Czechoslovakia and has done nothing to alleviate the situation. There are restrictions on equal opportunity for all citizens to pursue their vocations; personal and political qualifications are required for certain categories of work, and often the party's approval is required. There is no recourse to courts or any independent body in cases of discrimination and injustice.

Document No. 20/ 1982: Education of Youths and Children

The state has a monopoly over education. It regiments the system of educating the young and uses the system for social manipulation; consequently, children do not feel an urgency for restoring human and civil rights. A system of discrimination operates against certain applicants for admission to secondary and higher education; political considerations are most important in selection, including the political orientation of parents. The child is in actuality a hostage of the state, because access to education is a powerful instrument of pressure. From an early age young people are subjected to political indoctrination and are given incomplete or distorted information. Religious education is almost totally suppressed.

Document No. 22/ 1982: The Situation in Prisons

Conditions in prisons should be investigated and legal measures introduced that would place the status and treatment of prisoners in accordance with international pacts on human and civil rights. There are numerous cases of gross mistreatment of inmates by prison authorities or guards, the refusal of medical care, and even some instances of death from exhaustion. Political prisoners should be separated from criminal ones and have the right to education and religious services.

Document No. 4/ 1983: A Contribution to the Discussion on the Economic Situation in Czechoslovakia

During 1981–1982 the economy underwent worsening stagnation. A smaller portion of national income was allocated for reinvestment, partly because of repayment of pre–1980

Western debts. The productivity of labor declined, investment fell by 4.6 percent (1981), 55 percent of enterprises did not complete construction plans (1982), and a negative trade balance appeared with the West and with socialist states. Industrial production in 1975–1981 only registered a 12 percent growth. The economy is dominated by heavy industry at the expense of consumer requirements; in 1982 the consumer sector actually declined. Compared to 1981, all of these negative trends worsened in 1982. The average worker and consumer suffer as a result.

Document No. 36/ 1983: On the Ecological Situation

The environment is rapidly deteriorating, and the authorities are not taking preventative steps. The forests in Bohemia and Moravia are gravely endangered. Many water sources are seriously contaminated. The excessive use of fertilizers and preservatives has eroded arable soil. Expenditure for environmental protection is much lower than in other industrialized countries. Major investments are still allocated to heavy industry – the leading polluter. The government fails to disclose many facts, and the public remains misinformed. If effective measures are not taken soon, the average health of the population will probably decline.

Document No. 42/ 1983: On Drug Abuse

Czechoslovak society has witnessed a dangerous rise in the use of narcotic drugs, particularly among young people, which leads to drug addiction. Official government bodies, such as the Ministry of Health, withhold information from the public about the seriousness of the problem. The number of drug addicts is estimated in the tens of thousands; young people aged 15–19 are especially affected. The consumption of alcohol has markedly increased, with that of unadulterated spirits more than double the 1960 figures.

The number of alcoholics is estimated at 300,000. Medicines containing narcotic substances (e.g., codeine) are freely sold on the open market. The drug problem is comparable to and perhaps surpasses that of the West. The state authorities must publicize the seriousness of the problem, otherwise the situation will continue to deteriorate.

Document No. 10/ 1984: On the Right to Work

The provisions of the ILO Convention No.111, which forbid discrimination on the basis of political or religious beliefs, are being violated, despite adoption of these stipulations in 1975. In the 1970s, hundreds of thousands of people lost their jobs because of their political beliefs. A new wave of job dismissals was instigated against Charter 77 sympathizers. In October 1978, the Supreme Court maintained that "moral and political quality" is a criterion in job selection. Virtually all important positions are filled by Communist Party sympathizers, regardless of professional qualifications. The right to work in a job for which one is qualified is a basic human right. If the authorities continue these discriminatory practices, the morale and initiative of the work force will decline.

Document No. 11/ 1984: The Right to History

Every nation has a right to its history and to contemplate and explore its past. History is the source of national doctrines, ideologies, and myths. The Prague authorities are manipulating and distorting the nation's past. Only historical works that conform to the official ideology are allowed. By manipulating the past, the regime seeks to control the future. The study of history is in great danger. Public access to archives is severely restricted, especially post-1918 material. Some historical periods are almost totally ignored – for example, medieval times. Historians are denied contact with Western colleagues. Capable historians have been dismissed, severely restricted in their research, or forced into exile. Existing historical methodology is made to conform to official ideology. As a result of these practices, the national historical memory is seriously threatened.

Document No. 14/ 1984: Health is an Integral Part of the Right to Life

The health care system, despite commendable achievements, is plagued by inadequate care and waste. Although the 1982 ratio of one doctor per 395 people was the second best in the world, many problems still exist. Health personnel are promoted according to political criteria and rarely by ability. The Ministry of Health suppresses valuable data on health needs. Medical research is controlled by inefficient five-year plans. The patient cannot choose a quality doctor because of rigid state controls. There is a shortage of personnel in many areas (e.g. geriatric care), medical equipment is outdated, and hygiene is often poor. As a result, the average health of citizens is somewhat worse than in other industrialized countries.

Document No. 20/ 1984: The Right to Information

The Prague government violates Article 19 of the International Covenant on Civil and Political Rights, which proclaims the right of free expression, including the right to seek, receive, and impart information of all kinds. The mass media is an "exclusive propaganda tool" of the Communist Party, involved in the systematic distortion and falsification of information and ideas. Several examples are cited: the media withheld information about the tragic famine at the time of the 1984 anniversary of the Ethiopian revolution and suppressed news about the outrage Poles felt when the Catholic priest Jerzy Popieluszko was murdered by the security police. Data about environmental and economic problems is suppressed or made to appear less severe. Journalists are manipulated by the party apparatus; those in opposition are dismissed, imprisoned, or forced into exile. Czechoslovak citizens are denied access to most Western publications, despite the Helsinki and Madrid obligations to secure freer flow of printed information. Czechoslovak citizens have a deep distrust of the media and have come to believe that the truth is the opposite of what is printed.

Document No. 5/ 1985: The Prague Appeal

This document was drafted as a letter to the 1985 peace congress in Amsterdam. Europe remains a divided continent, and this division contributes to world tension and threatens international peace. A gradual dissolution of the two blocs must be initiated. The chances for this are not as unfavorable as they may appear. The Conference on European Security and Cooperation, in which all states in principle are equally represented, is a crucial step in the right direction. The Helsinki Final Act provides a framework through which European groups and individuals could oblige their governments to take steps toward ensuring peace – including proposals for disarmament and the creation of nuclear free zones. The question of German reunification must be reconsidered. The superpowers must negotiate for the eventual withdrawal of all outside forces from Europe. The ultimate goal must be the creation of a united Europe of free, self-determining nation-states. This is the genuine desire of the majority of Europeans.

Document No. 7/ 1985: Suggestions Concerning Legislative Reform

In September 1984 the Czechoslovak government ratified the Concluding Document of the Madrid session of the Helsinki Final Act follow-up conferences. The document proclaims the right of every individual to "know his rights and duties, and to act accordingly." To comply with this document and to avoid further violations, the Czechoslovak legal code needs to be reformed. In 1968 legislation gave constitutional courts the power to judge the validity of laws, and yet such courts do not exist. The legislation denying travel permits to persons "whose journey abroad will not be in harmony with the interests of the state" violates the right of free travel. Legislation permitting government control over various church activities violates the freedom of religion. Laws allowing the government to "suppress facts which clash with important interests of the state's domestic or foreign policy" often violate freedom of speech. Provisional legislation from 1968 forbidding "disturbances of the peace" often infringes on the right to free assembly. The chartists cite other abuses and call for immediate legislative reform.

Index

Edwards Brothers Malloy
Thorofare, NJ USA
August 25, 2014